INSTANT WALL A
VINTAGE PATTERNS

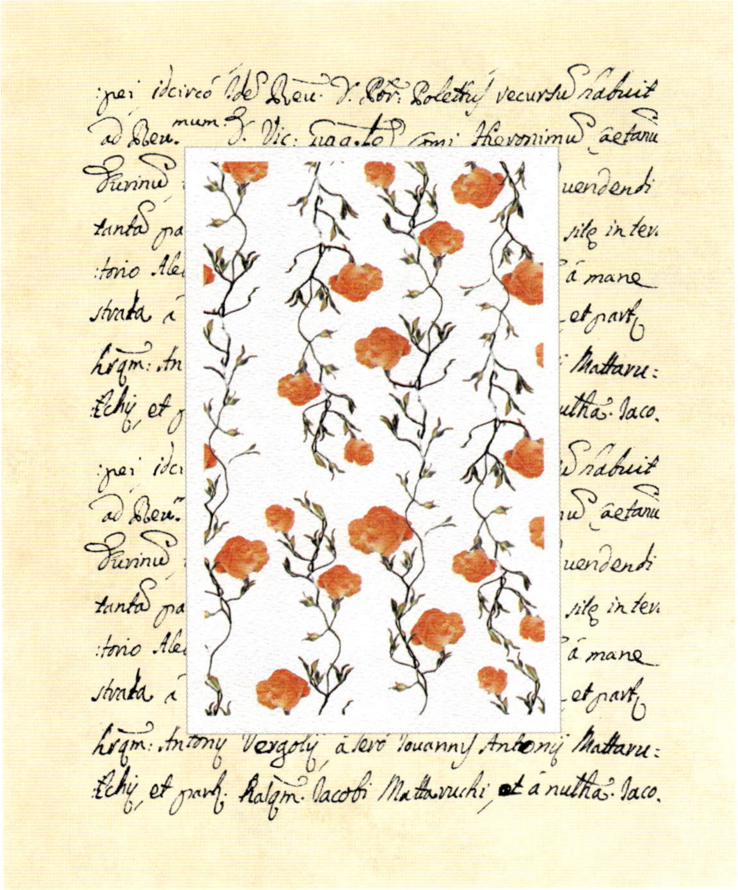

45 READY-TO-FRAME TEXTILE PRINTS FOR YOUR HOME DÉCOR

Adams Media
New York London Toronto Sydney New Delhi

adamsmedia
Adams Media
An Imprint of Simon & Schuster, Inc.
57 Littlefield Street
Avon, Massachusetts 02322

First Adams Media trade paperback edition DECEMBER 2017

Manufactured in the United States of America

10 9 8 7 6 5 4 3 2 1

ISBN 978-1-5072-0593-8

INTRODUCTION

Today, beautifully patterned textile prints are showing up everywhere you look—from popular design magazines and websites to the walls of your friends' living rooms and kitchens. And now, instead of having to choose between one or two expensive prints, you can choose from the forty-five beautiful prints found within the pages of *Instant Wall Art: Vintage Patterns* to personalize your own walls!

Spanning a variety of cultures and time periods, these prints are an eclectic mix of bright colors and subtle flair, all with a global twist. Now, with images ranging from Moroccan textiles to Japanese screens to French fabrics, you're sure to find something in this book that speaks to your design aesthetic. These vintage prints measure 8" × 10" and will fit in a standard mat and frame once removed from the book at the perforated edge. So choose the prints you love, hang them on your walls, and enjoy their elegance in your own home year round!

THE PRINTS

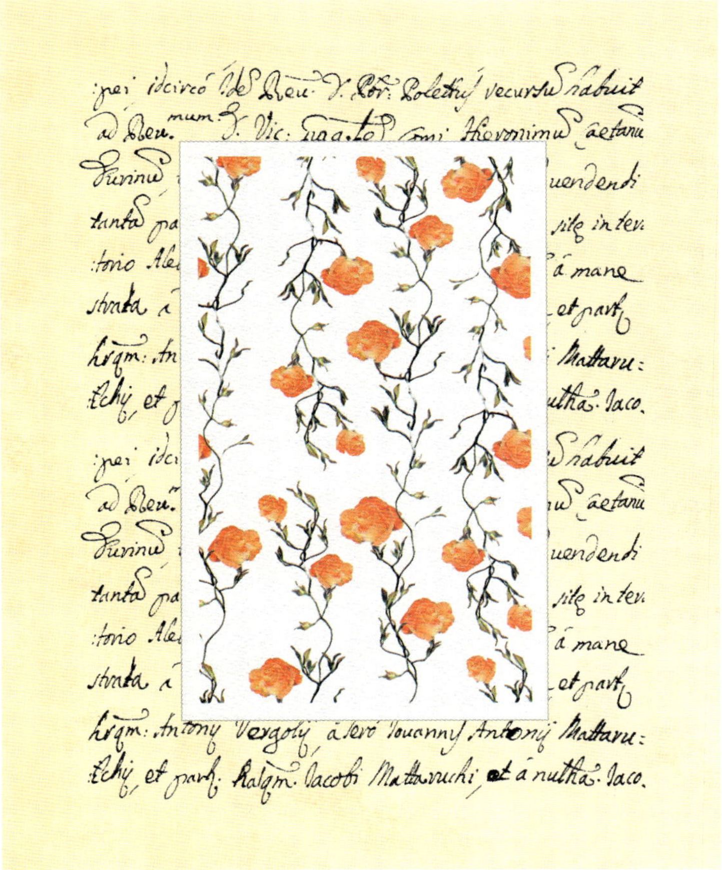

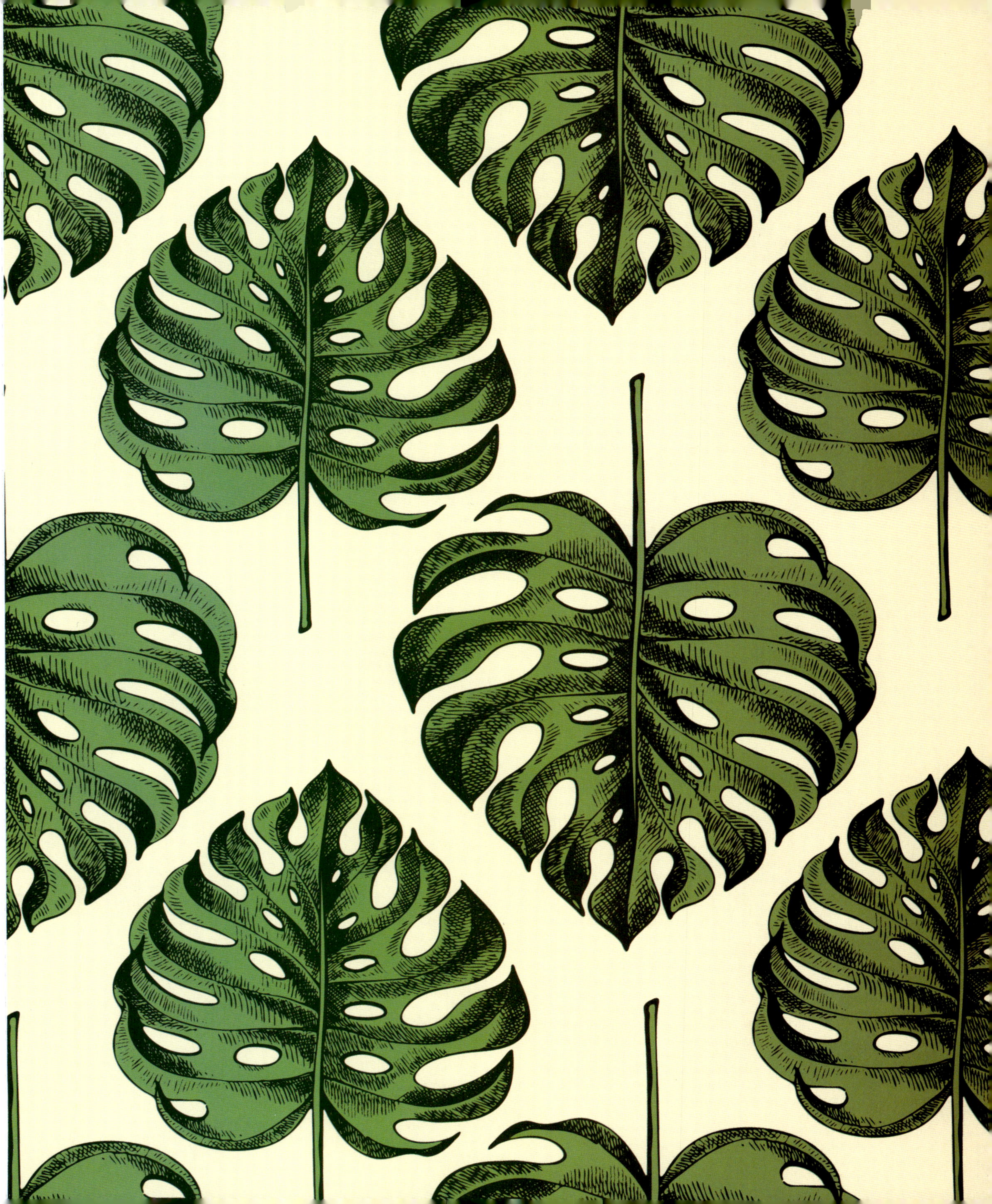

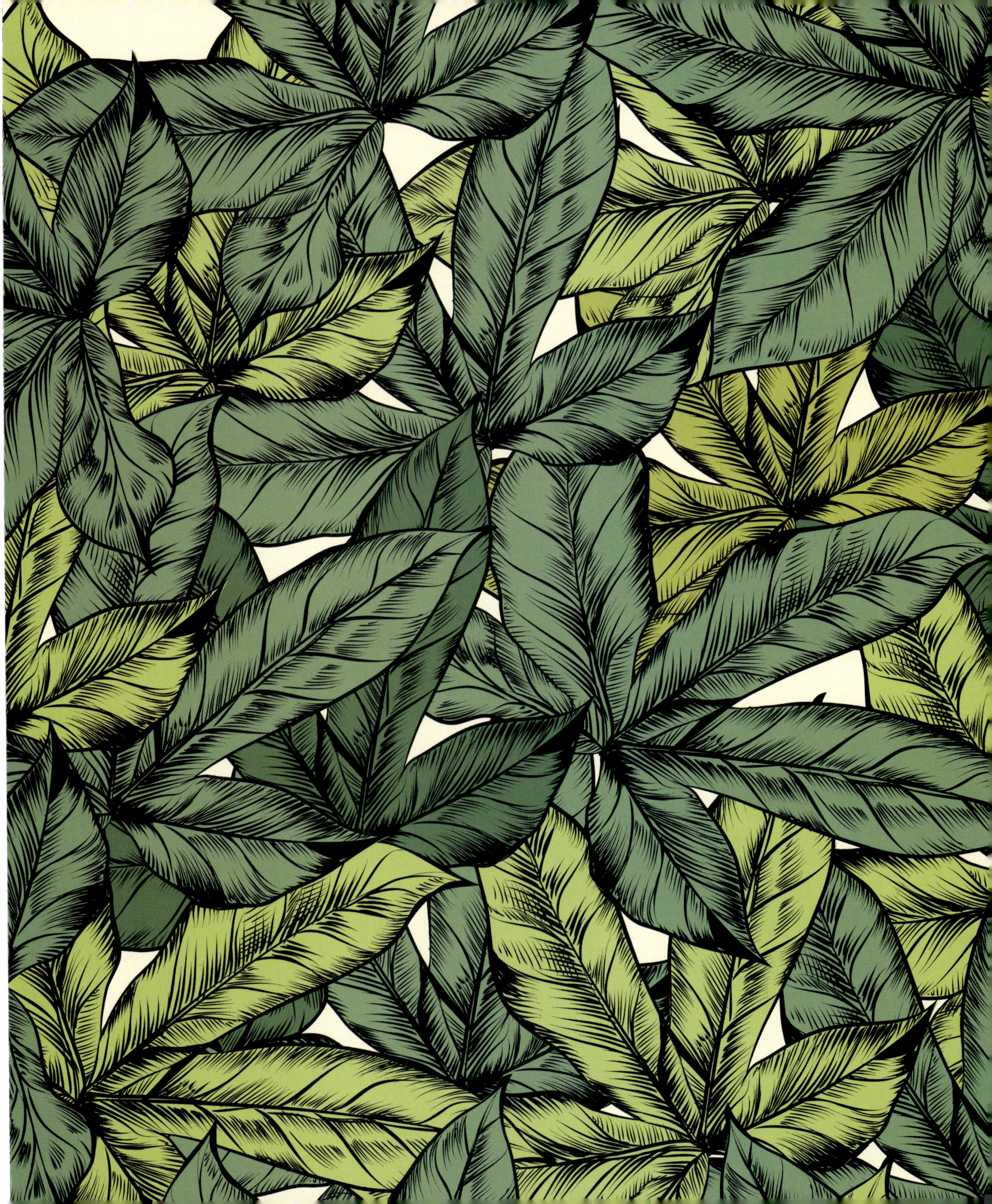

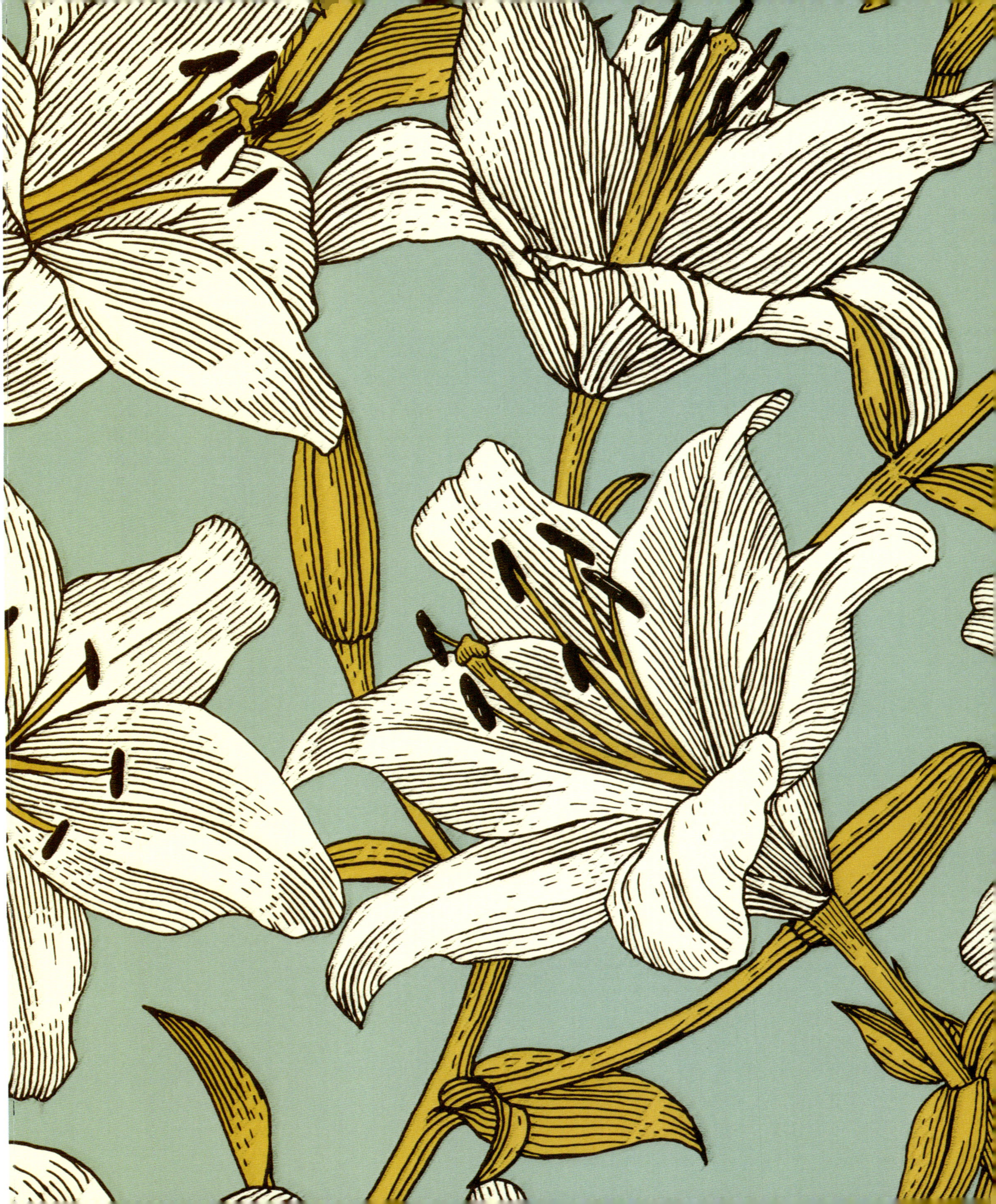

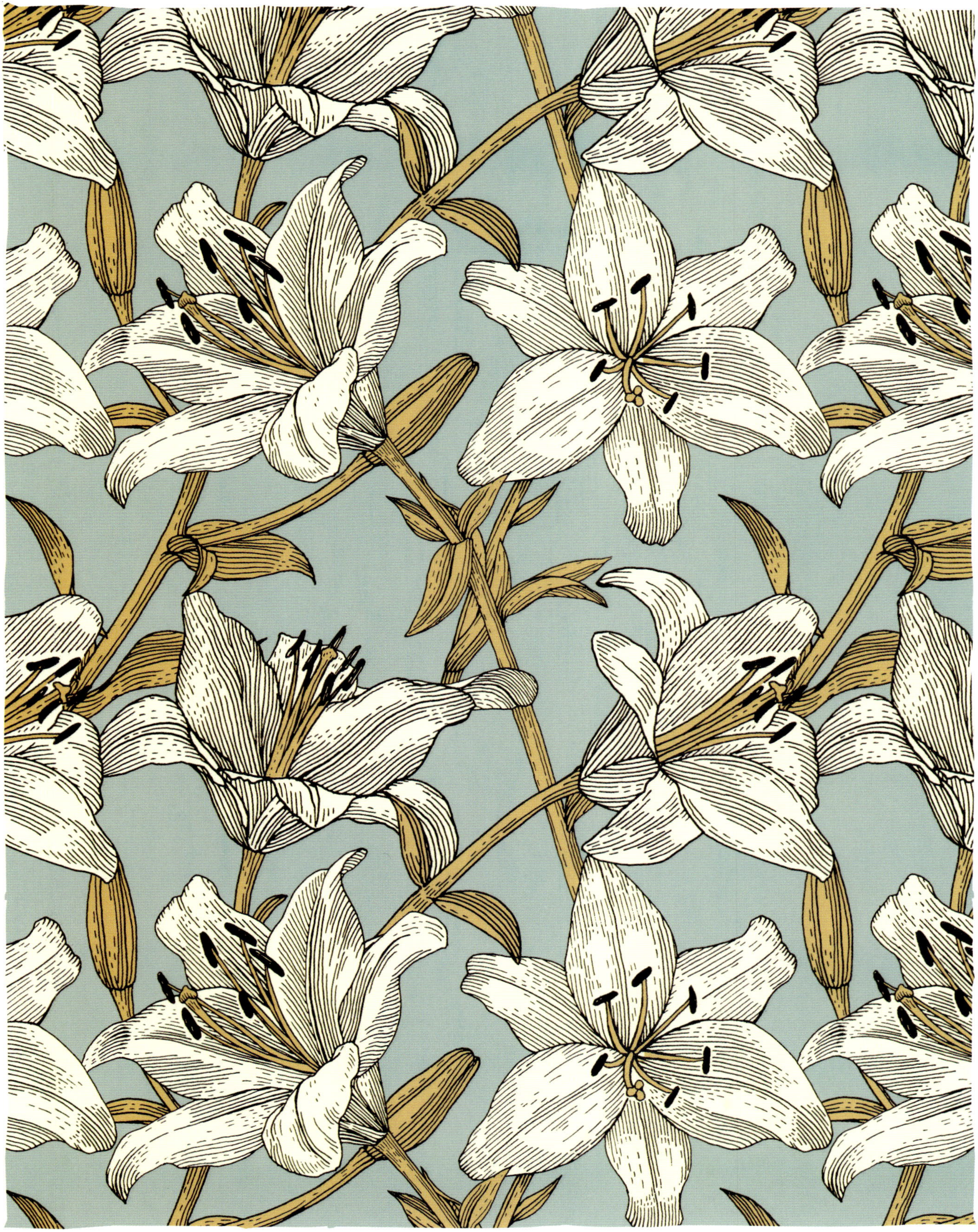

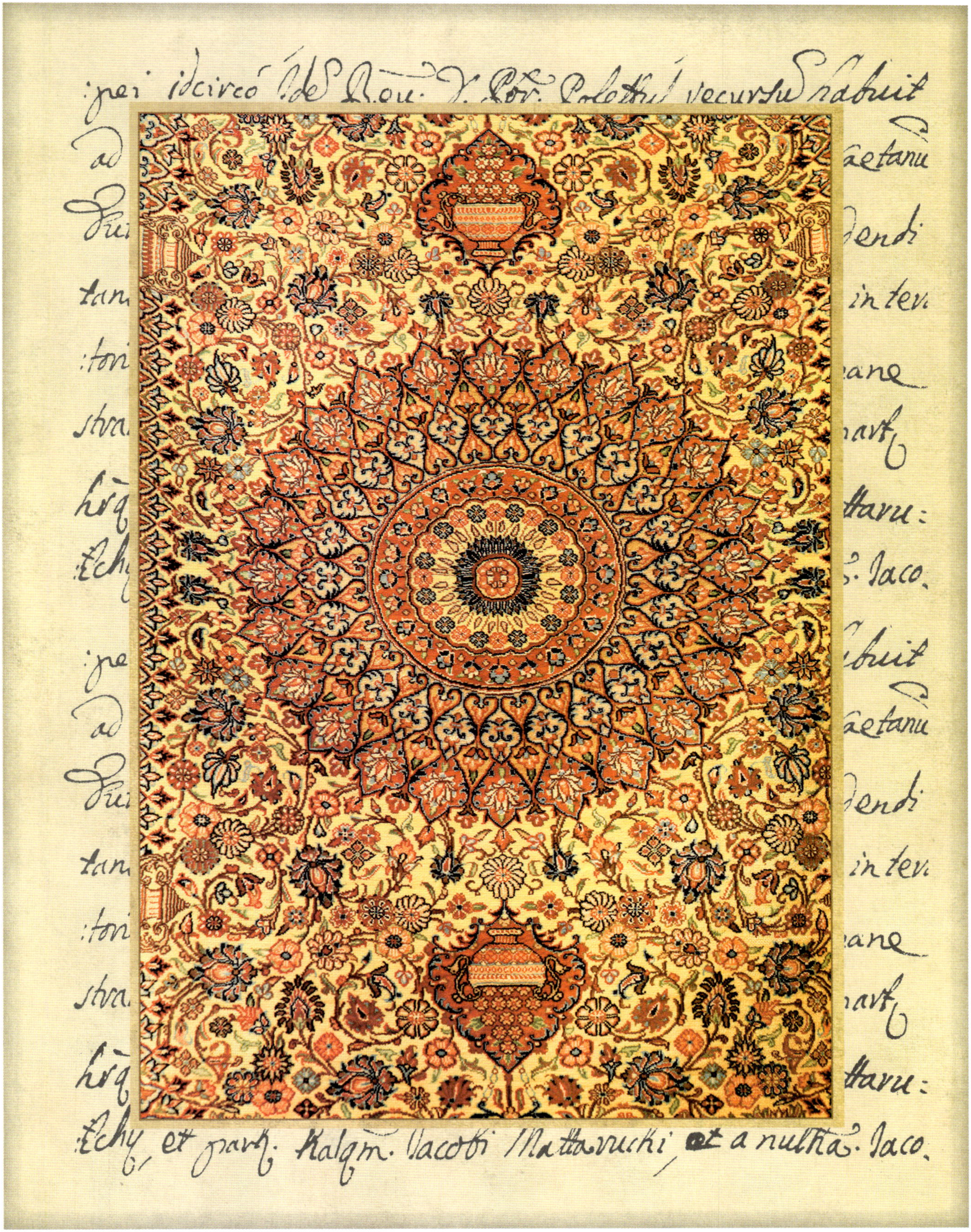

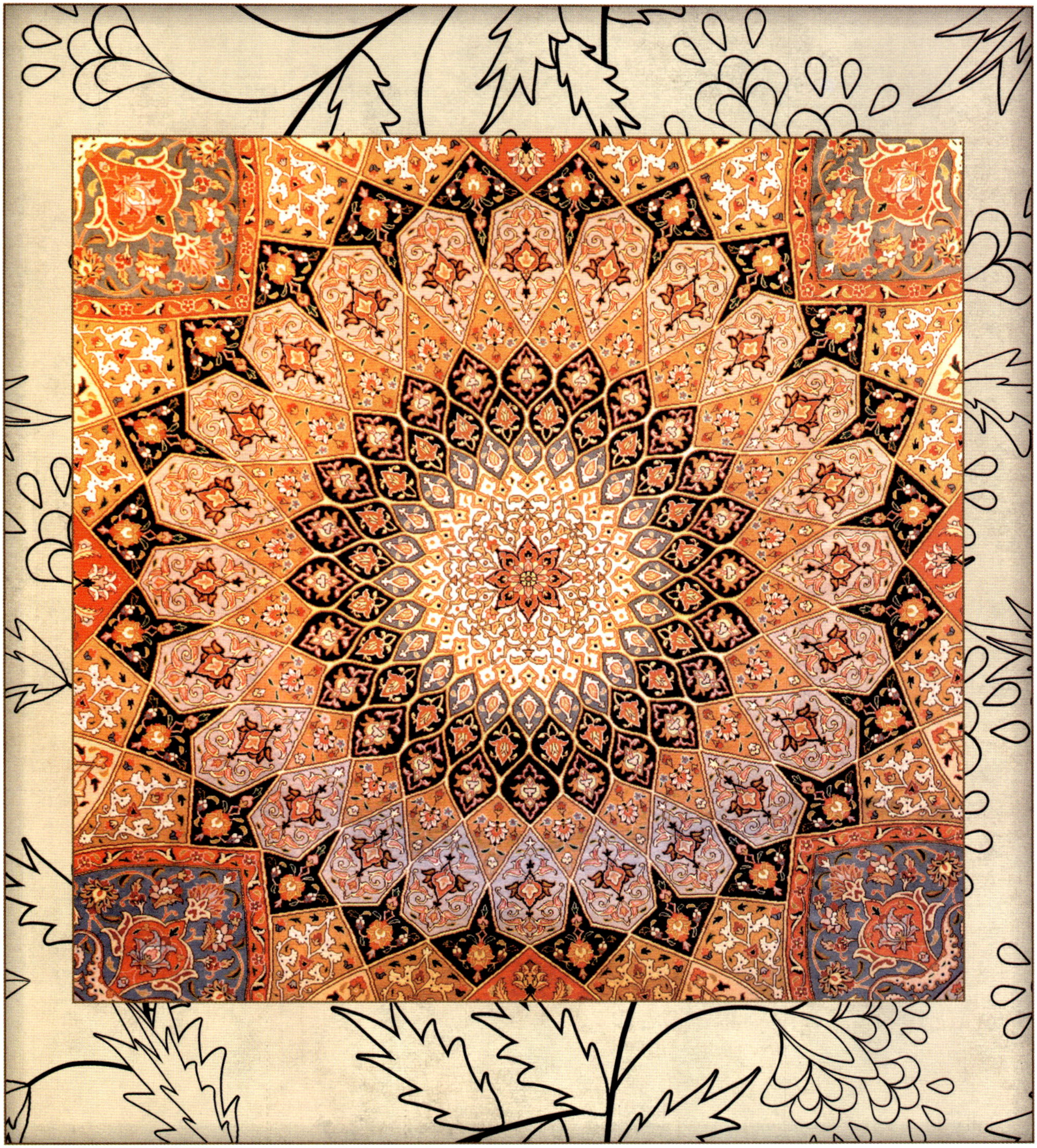

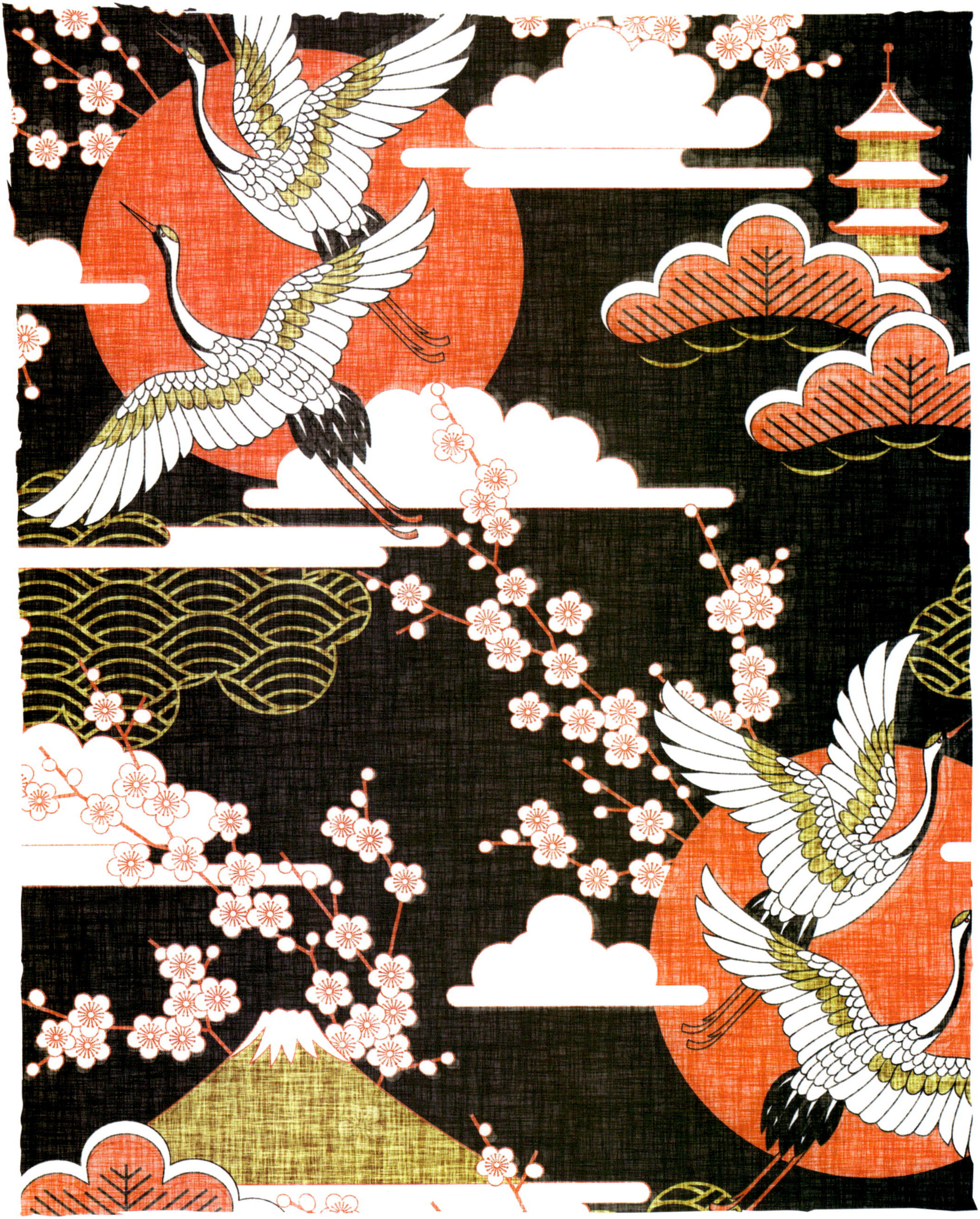

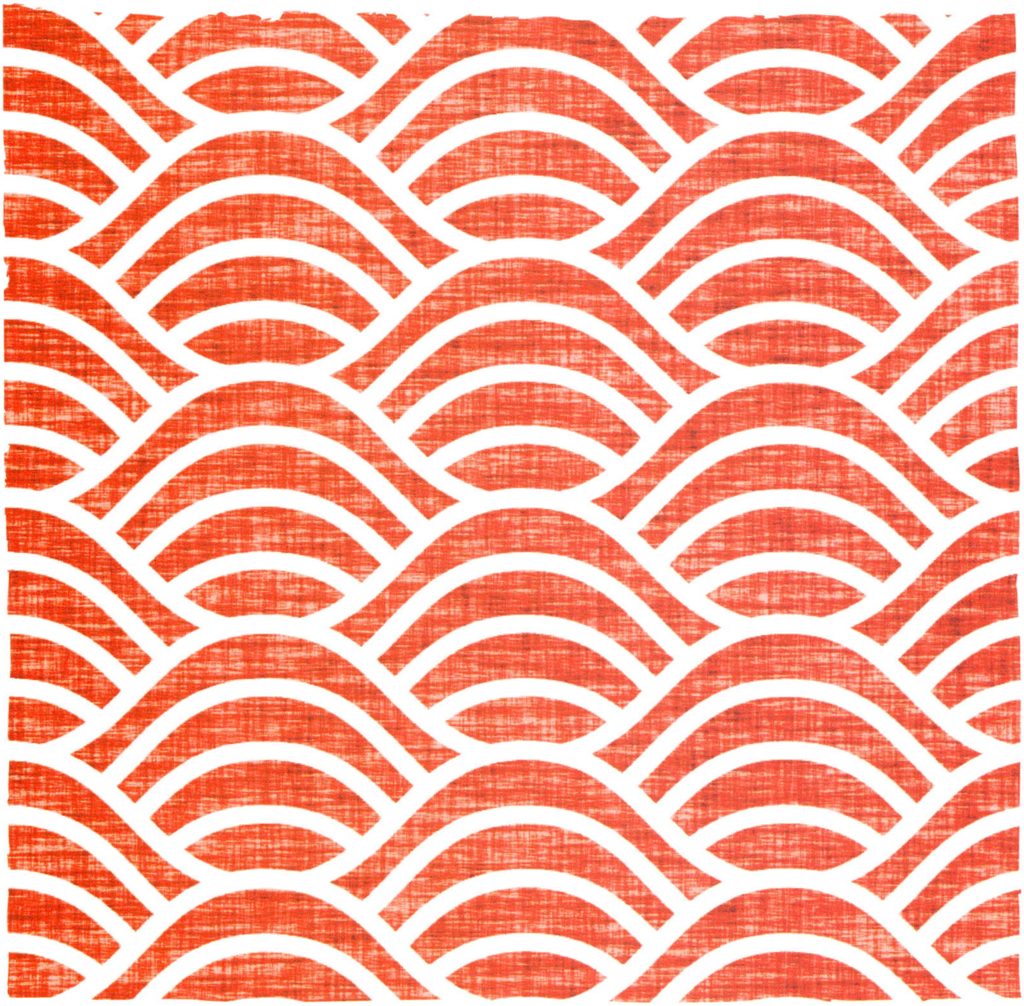

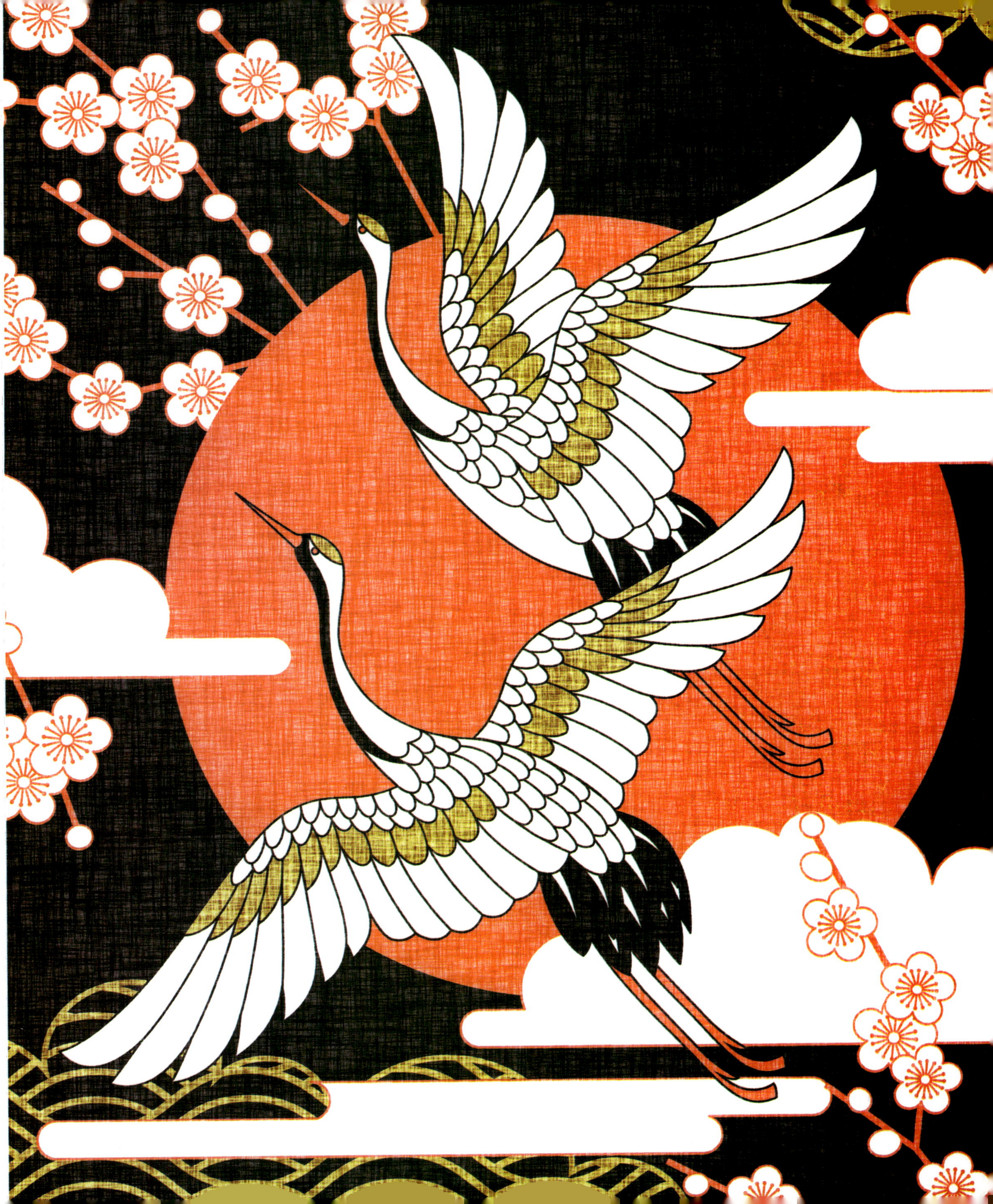

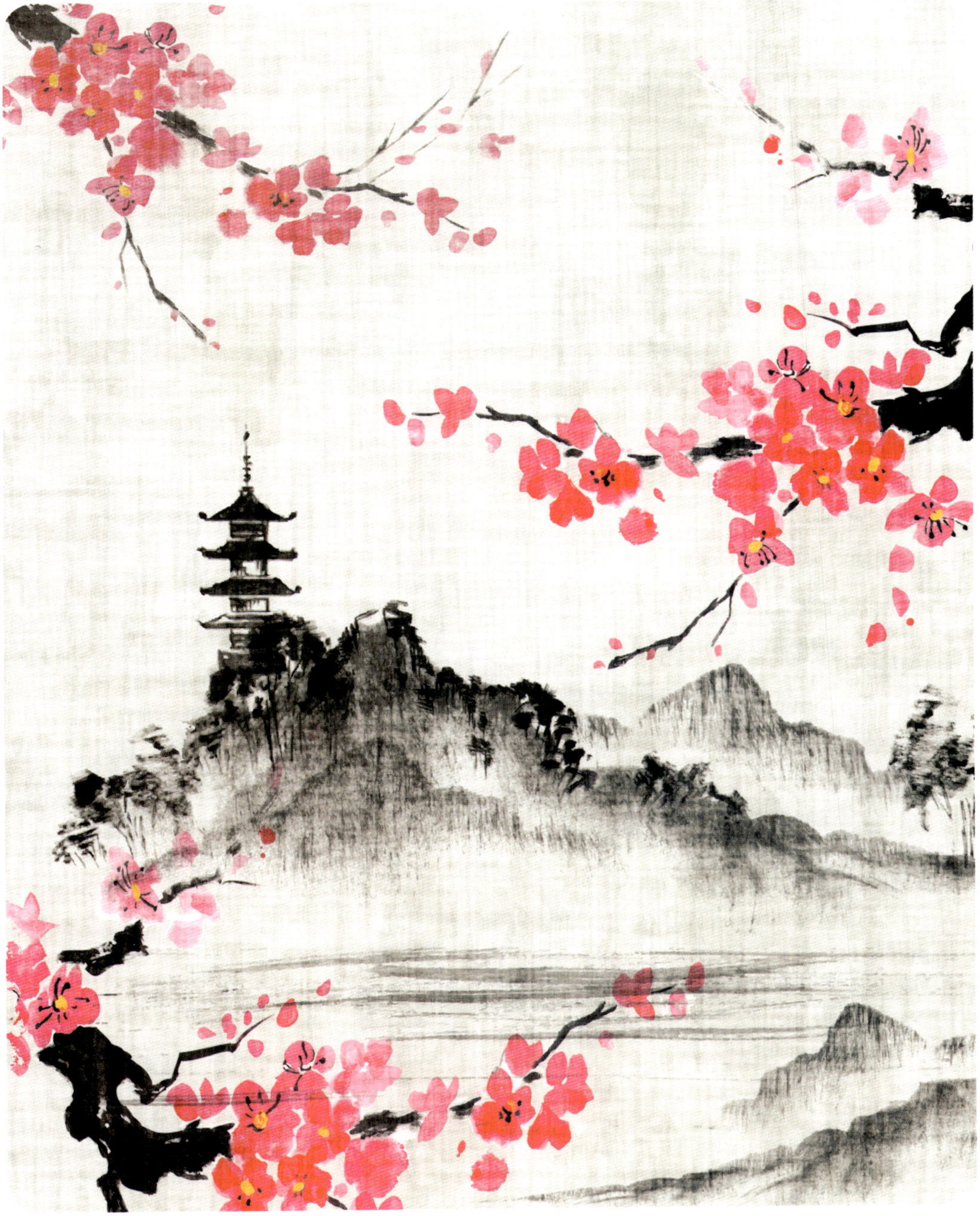

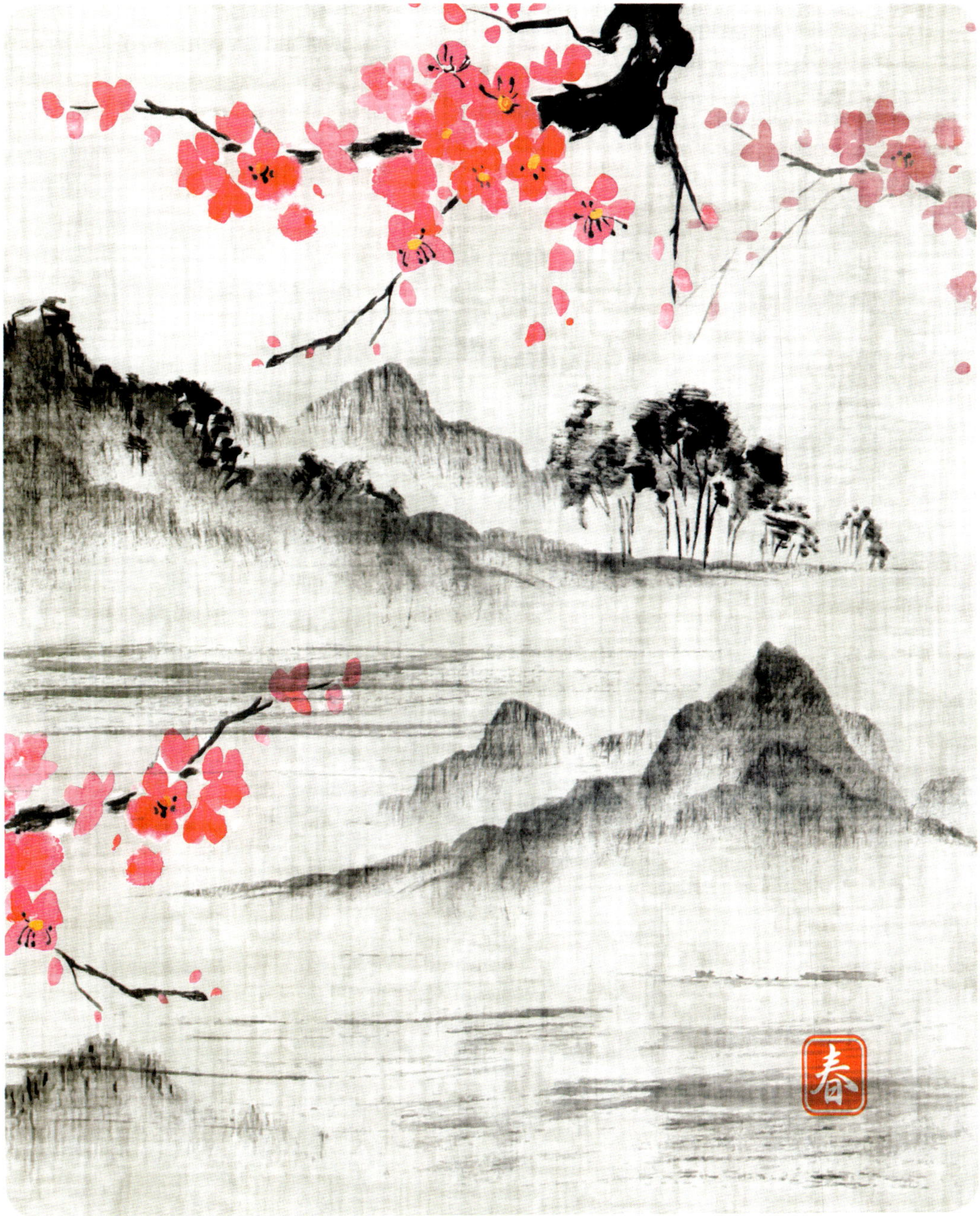
春

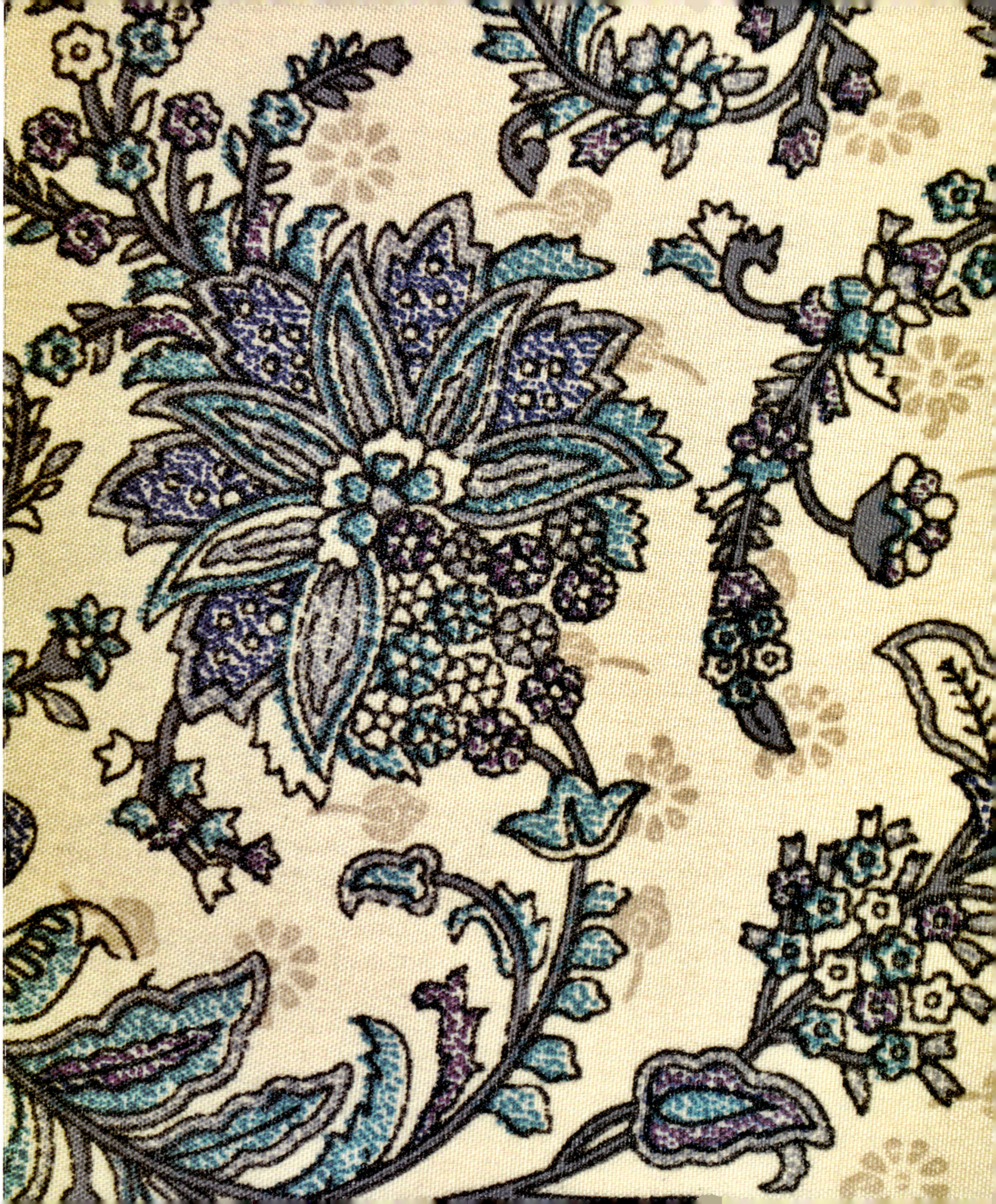

Image © Dreamstime/Oleksii Sergieiev

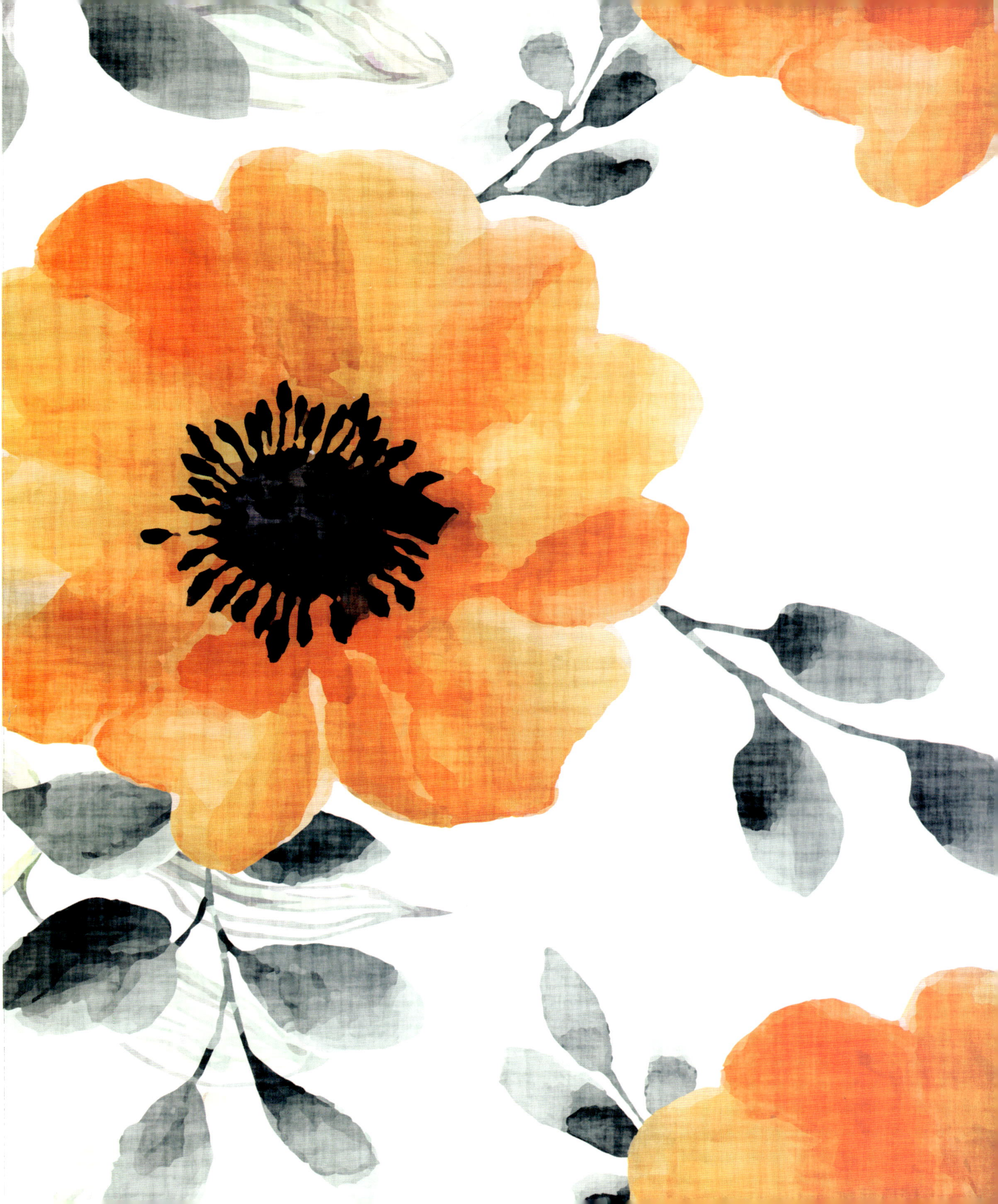

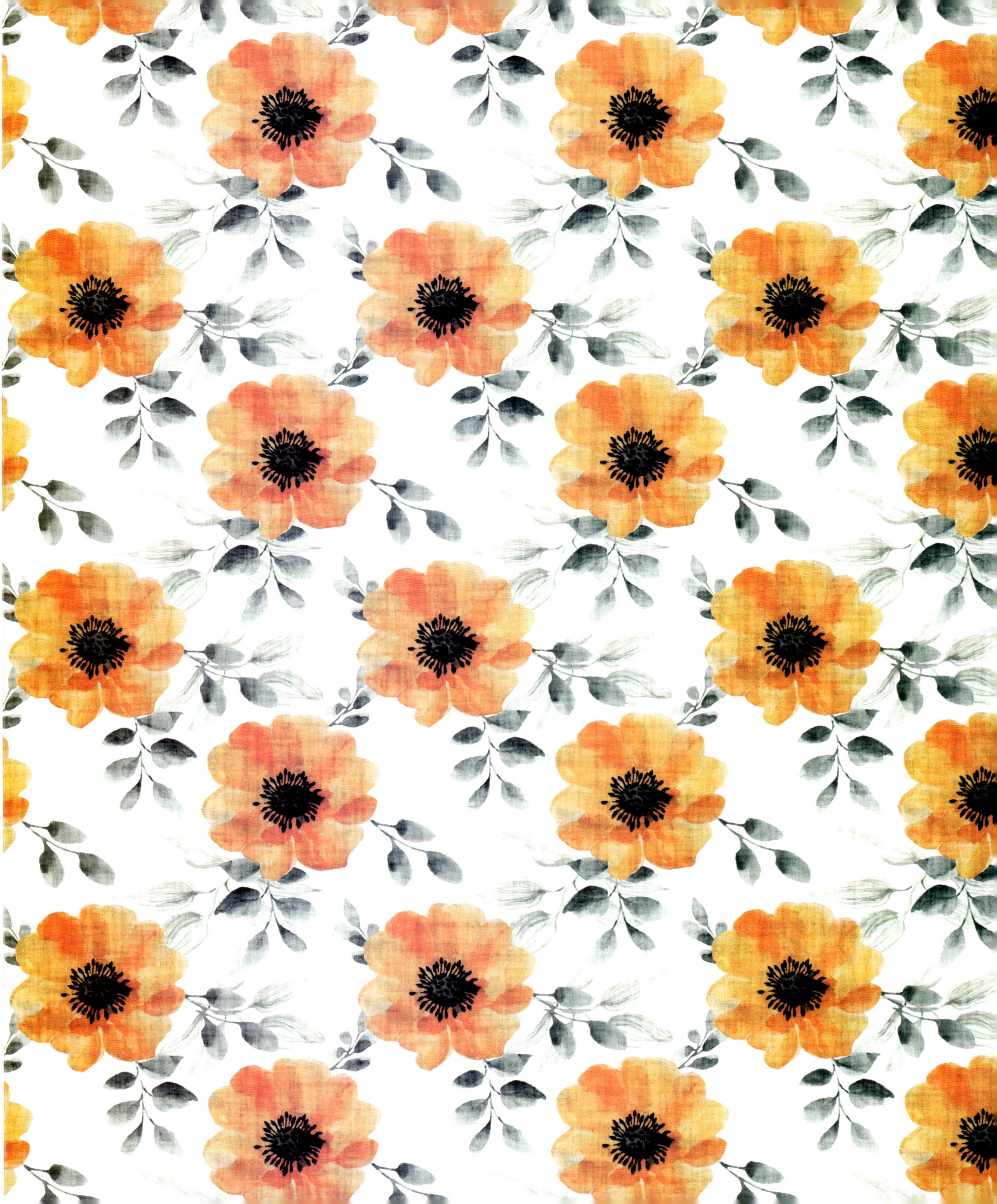

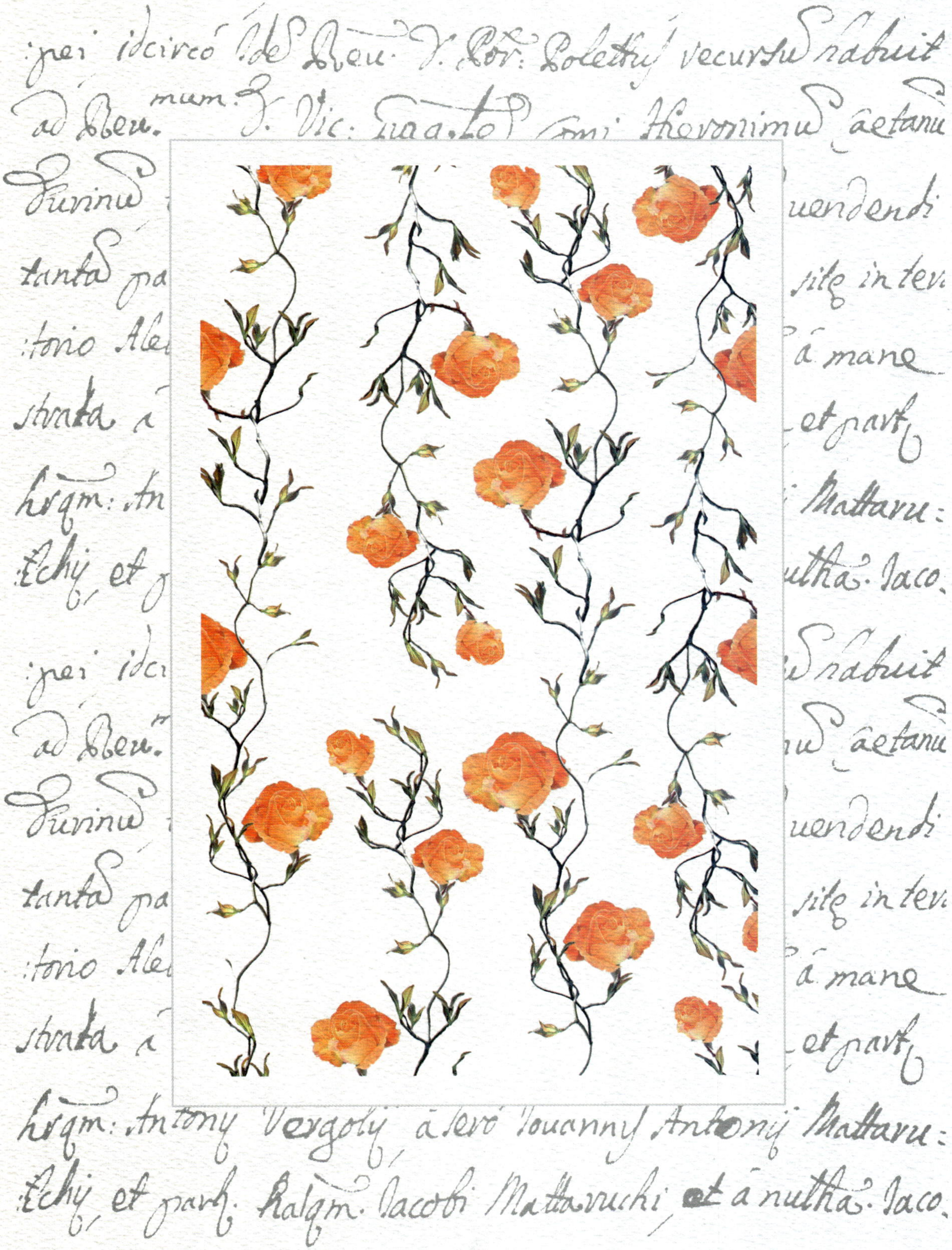

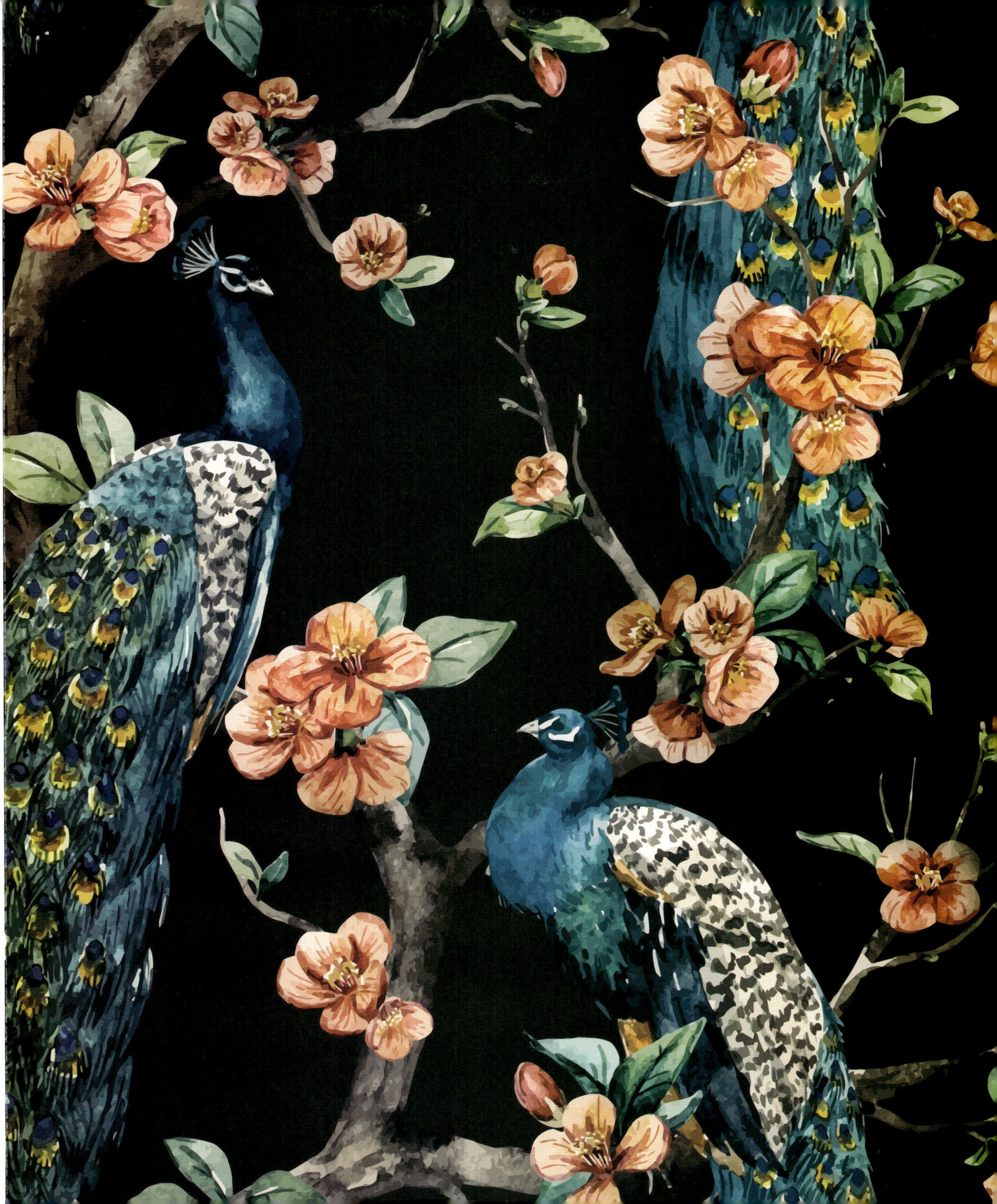

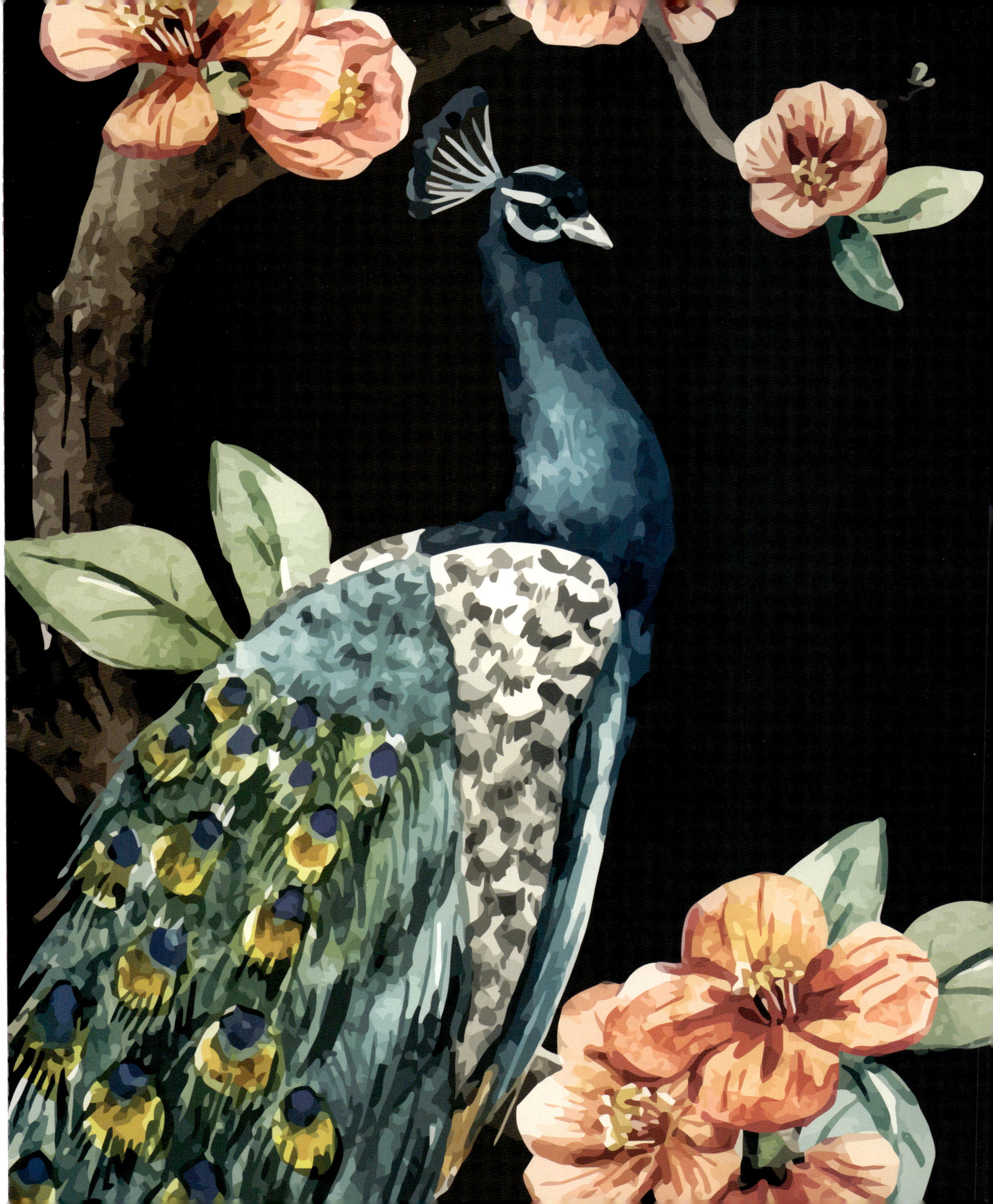

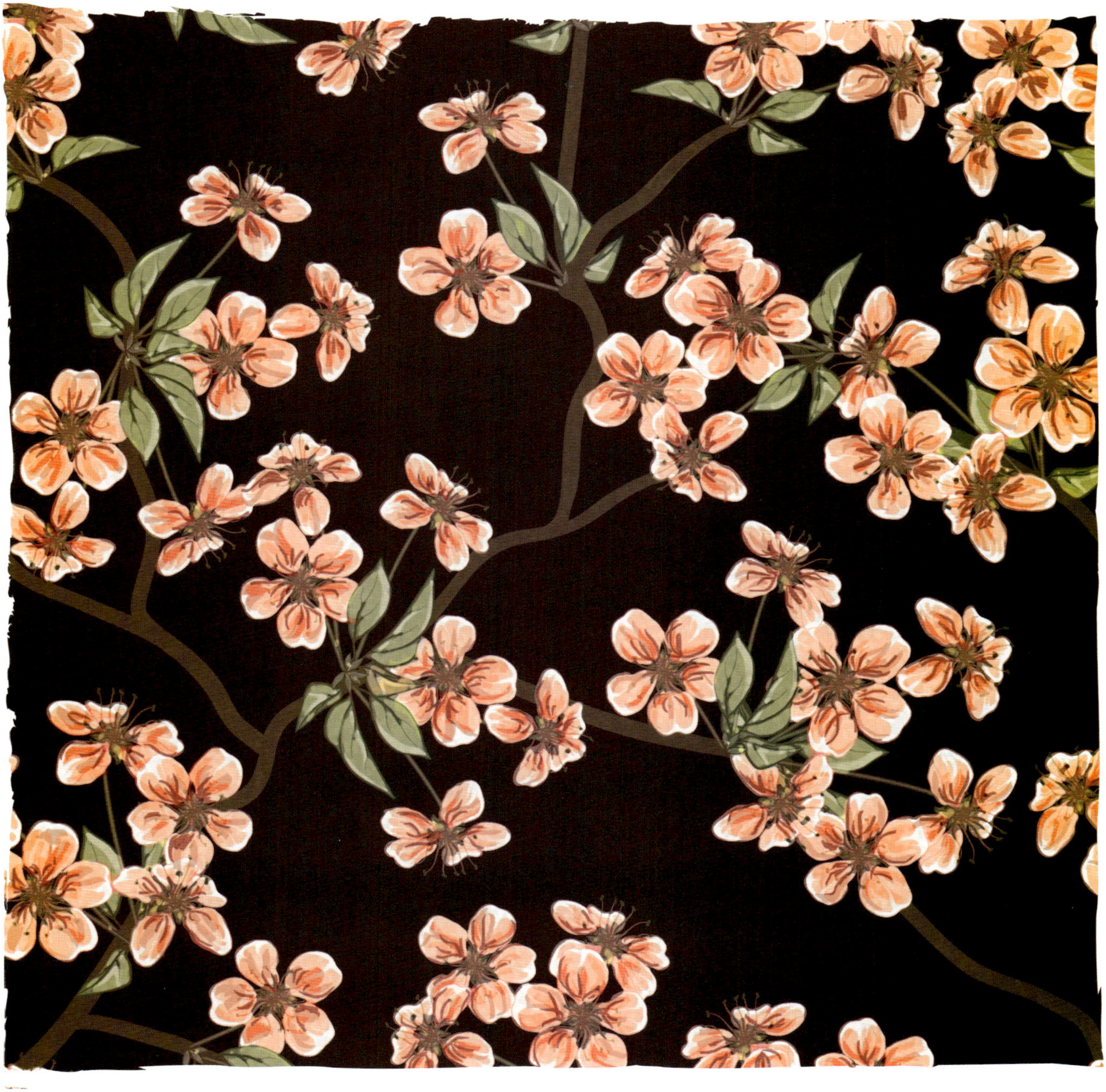

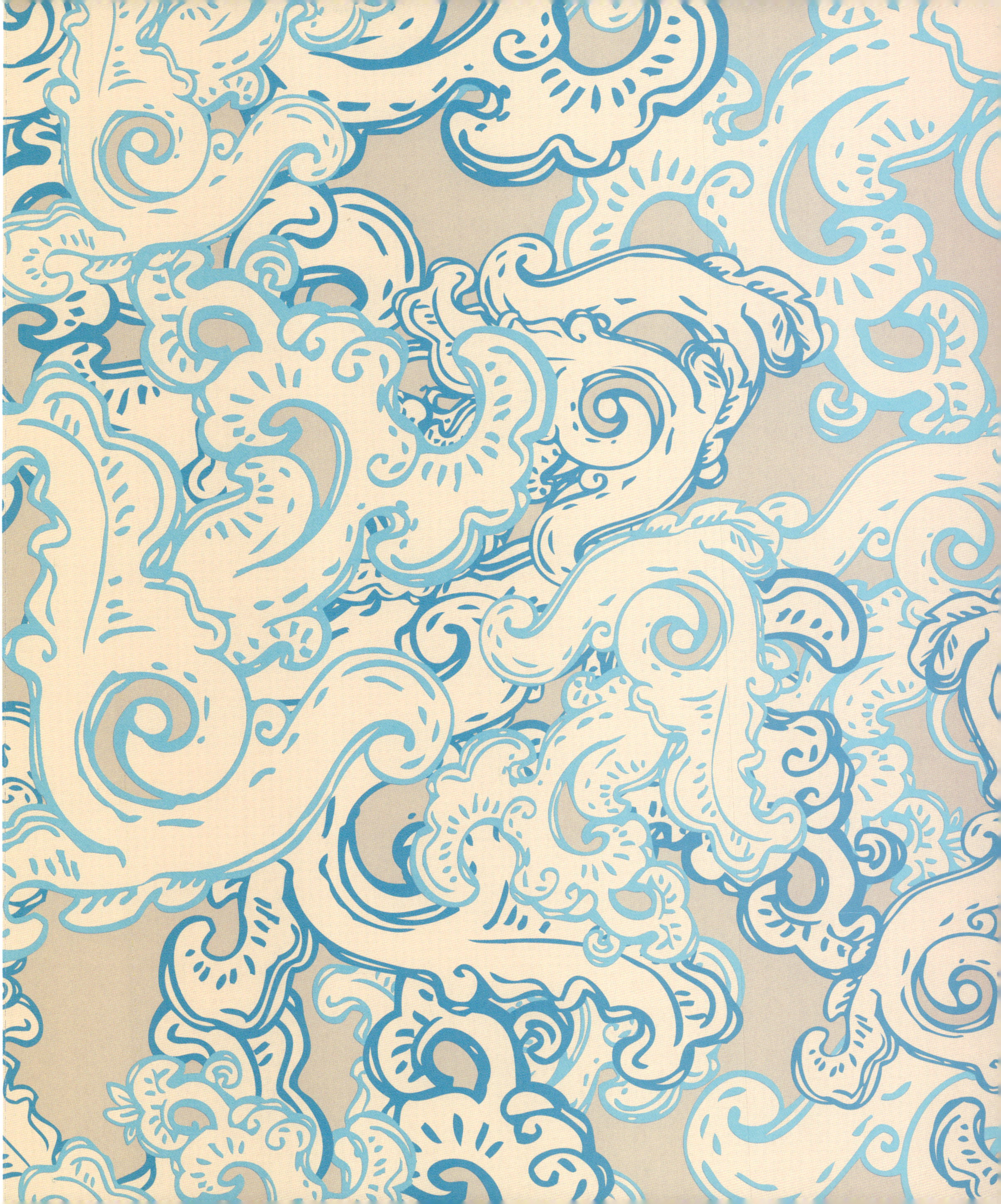

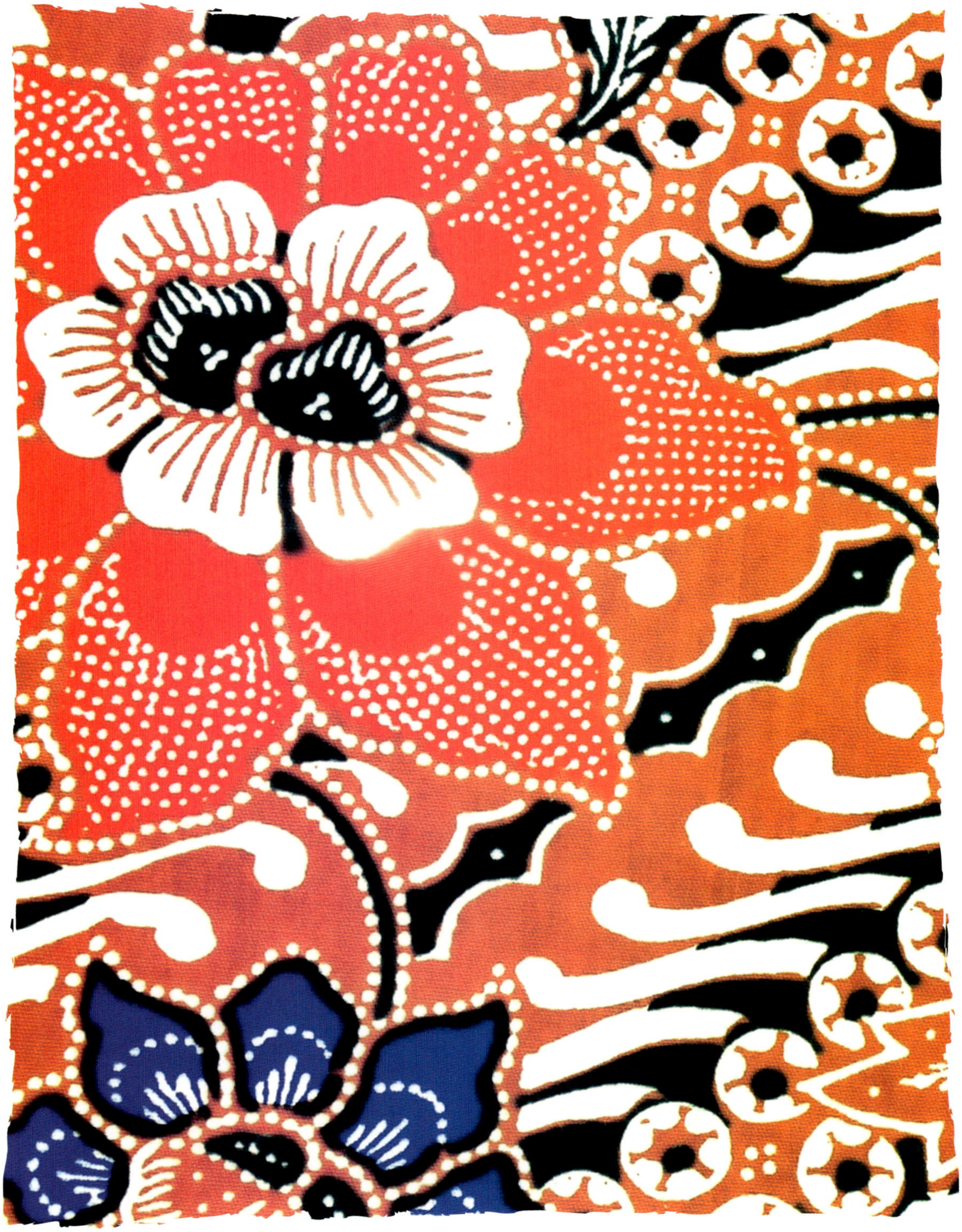

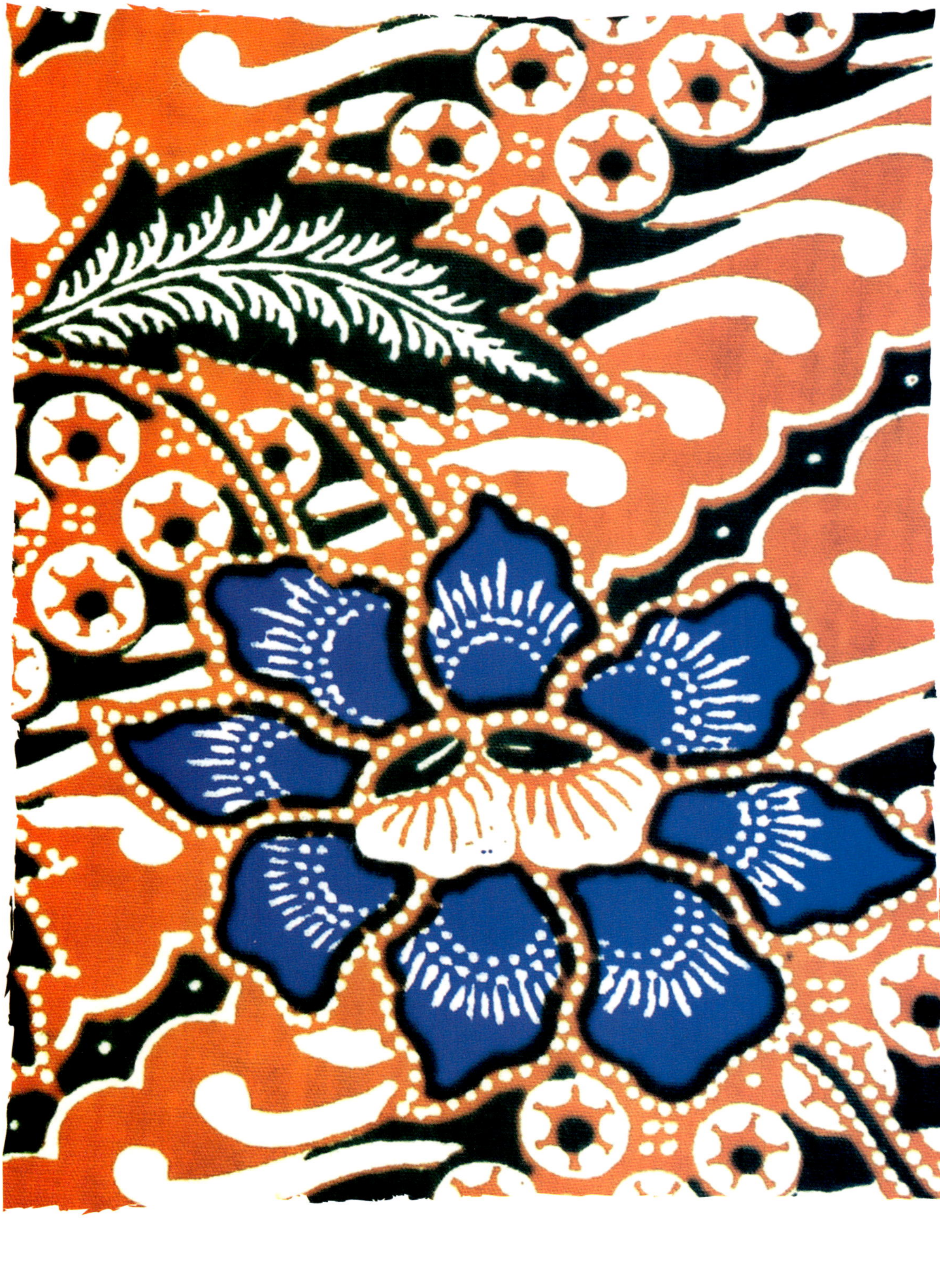

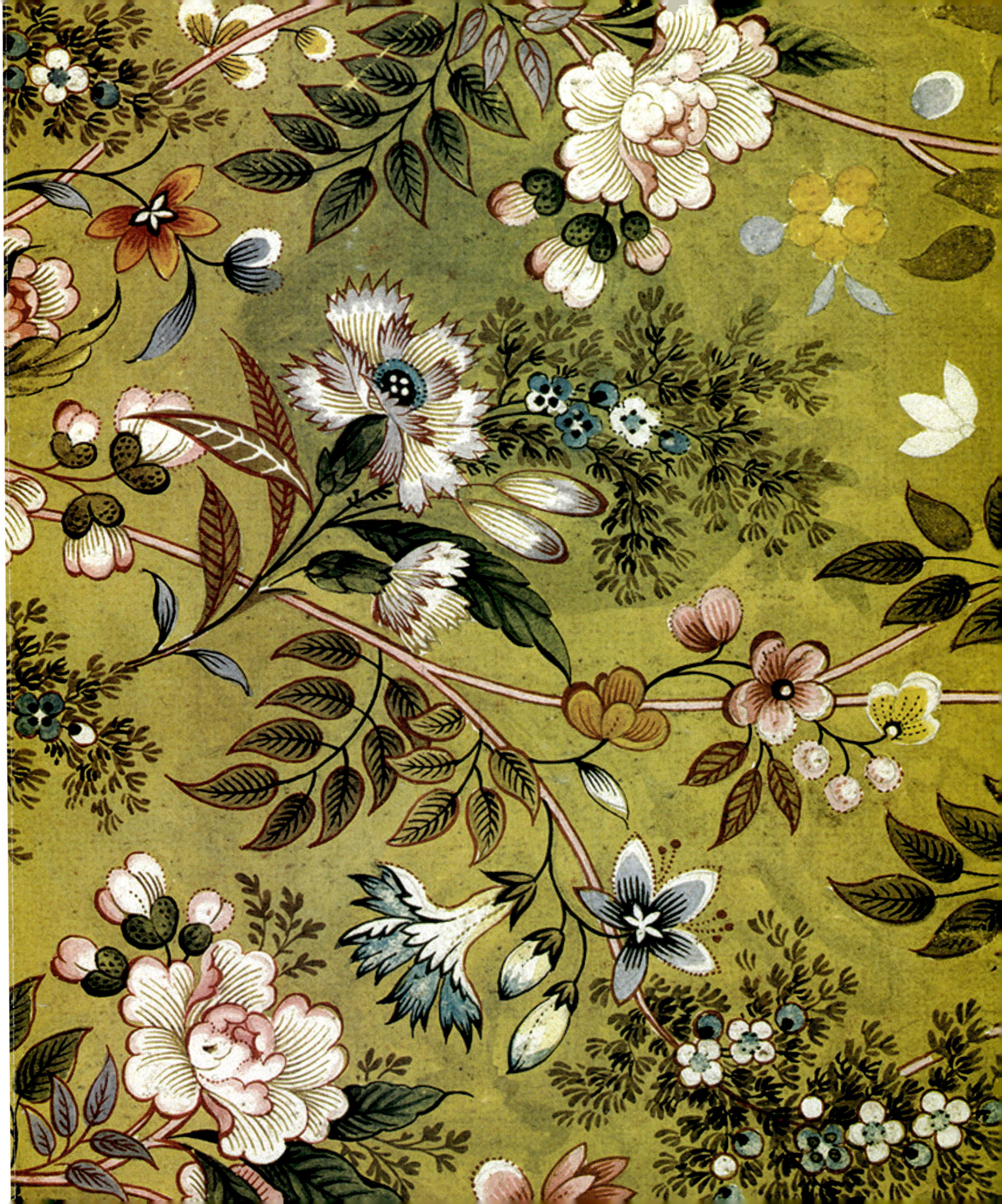

Image © Dreamstime/Jodielee

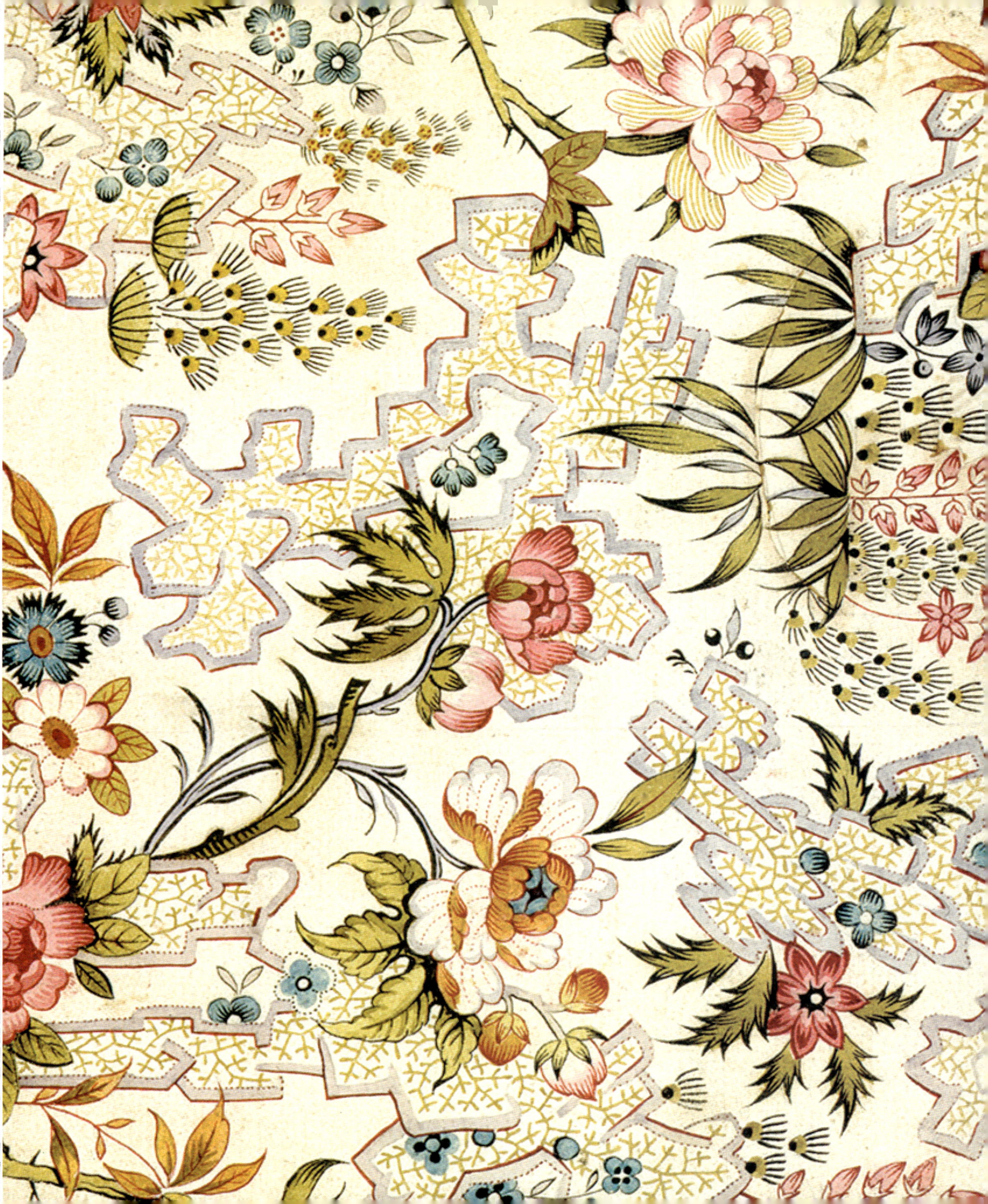

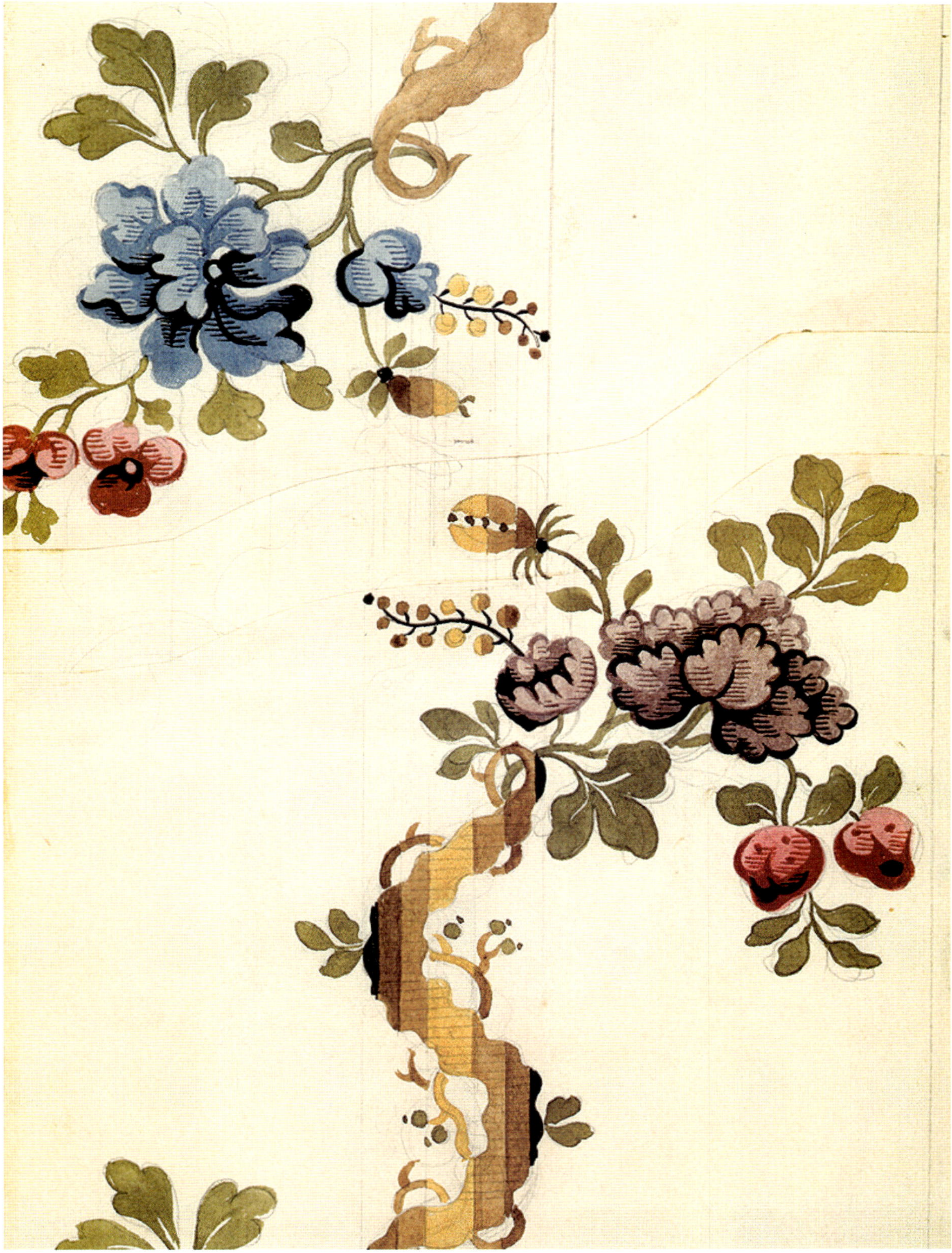

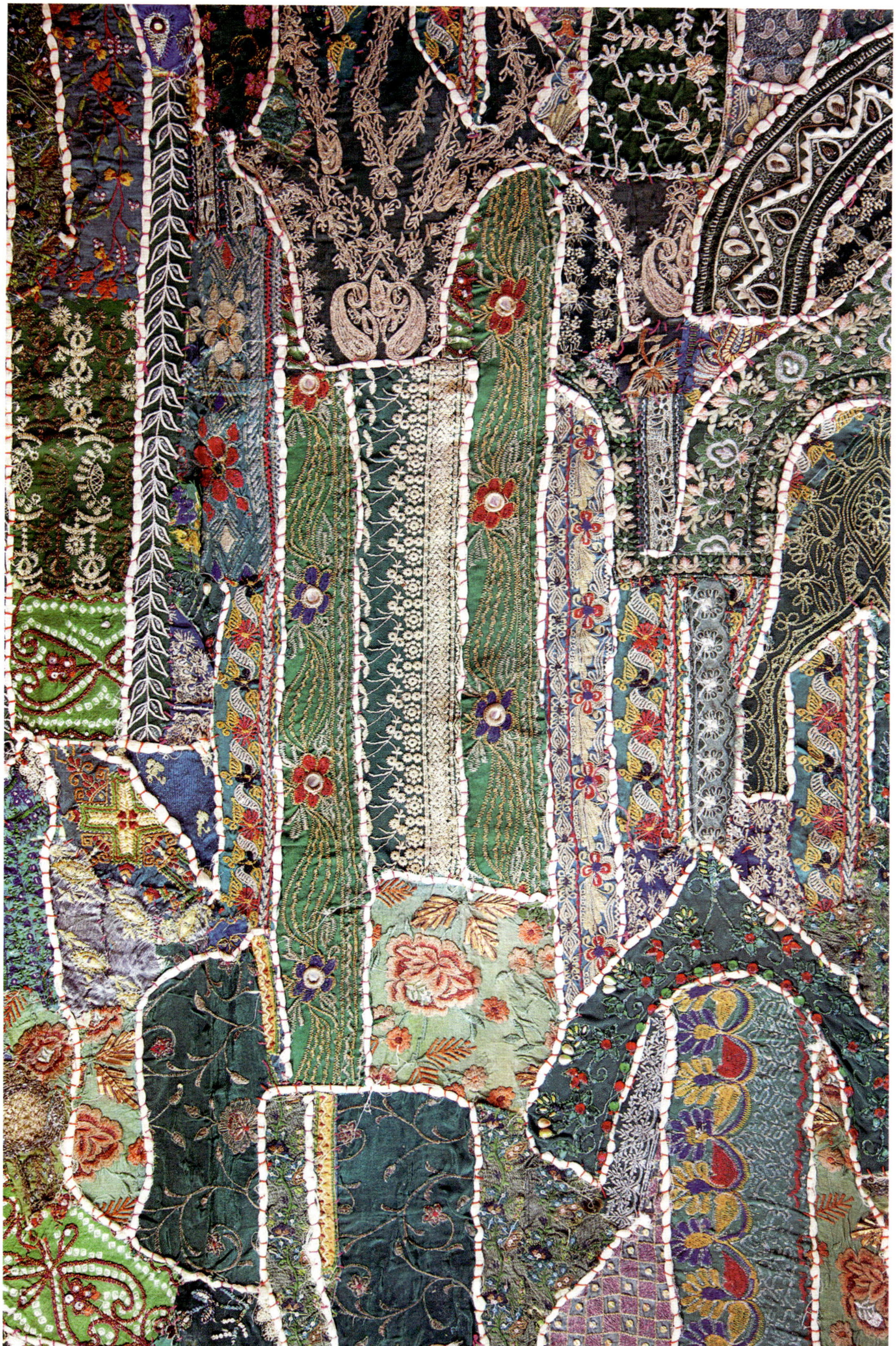

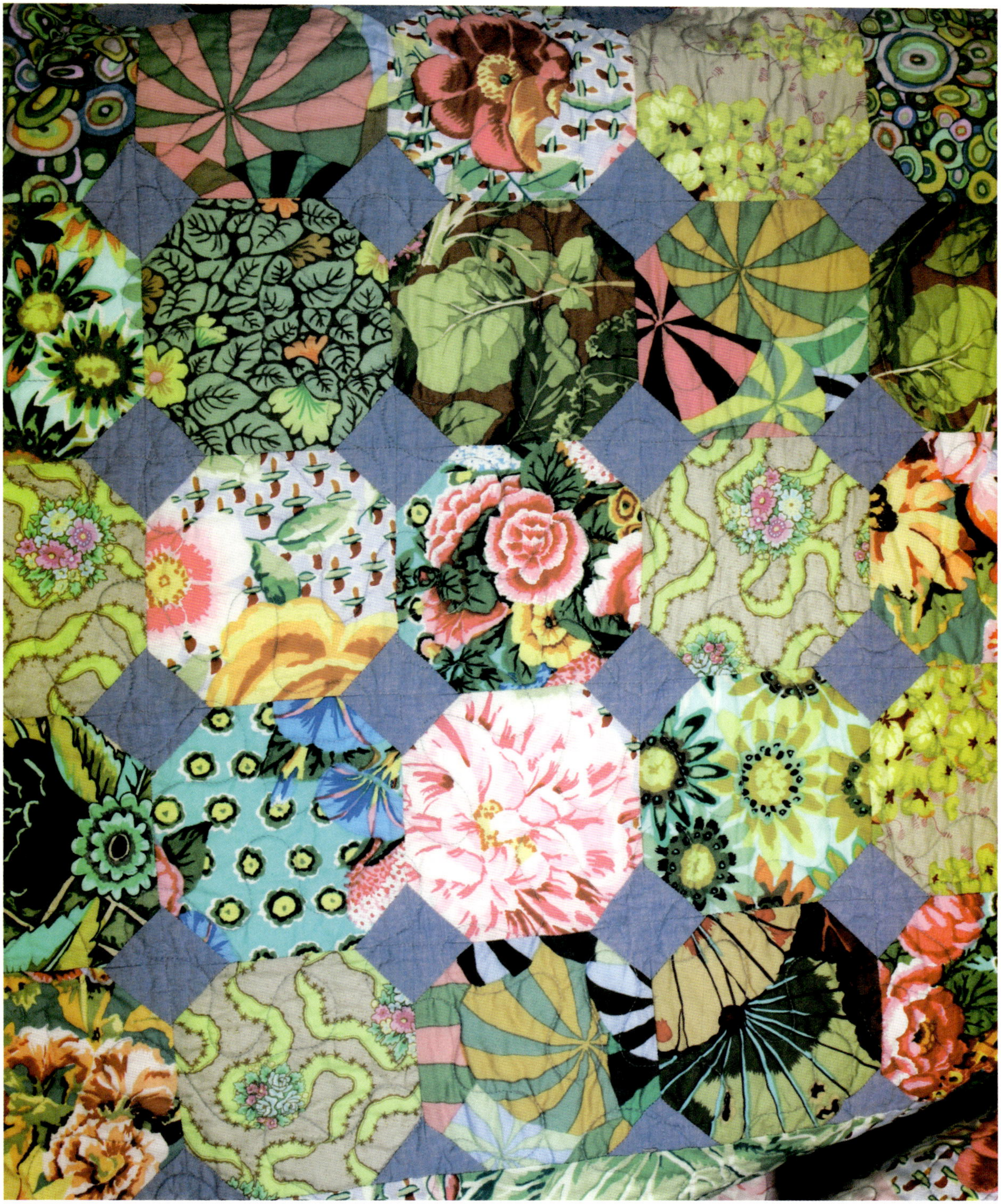

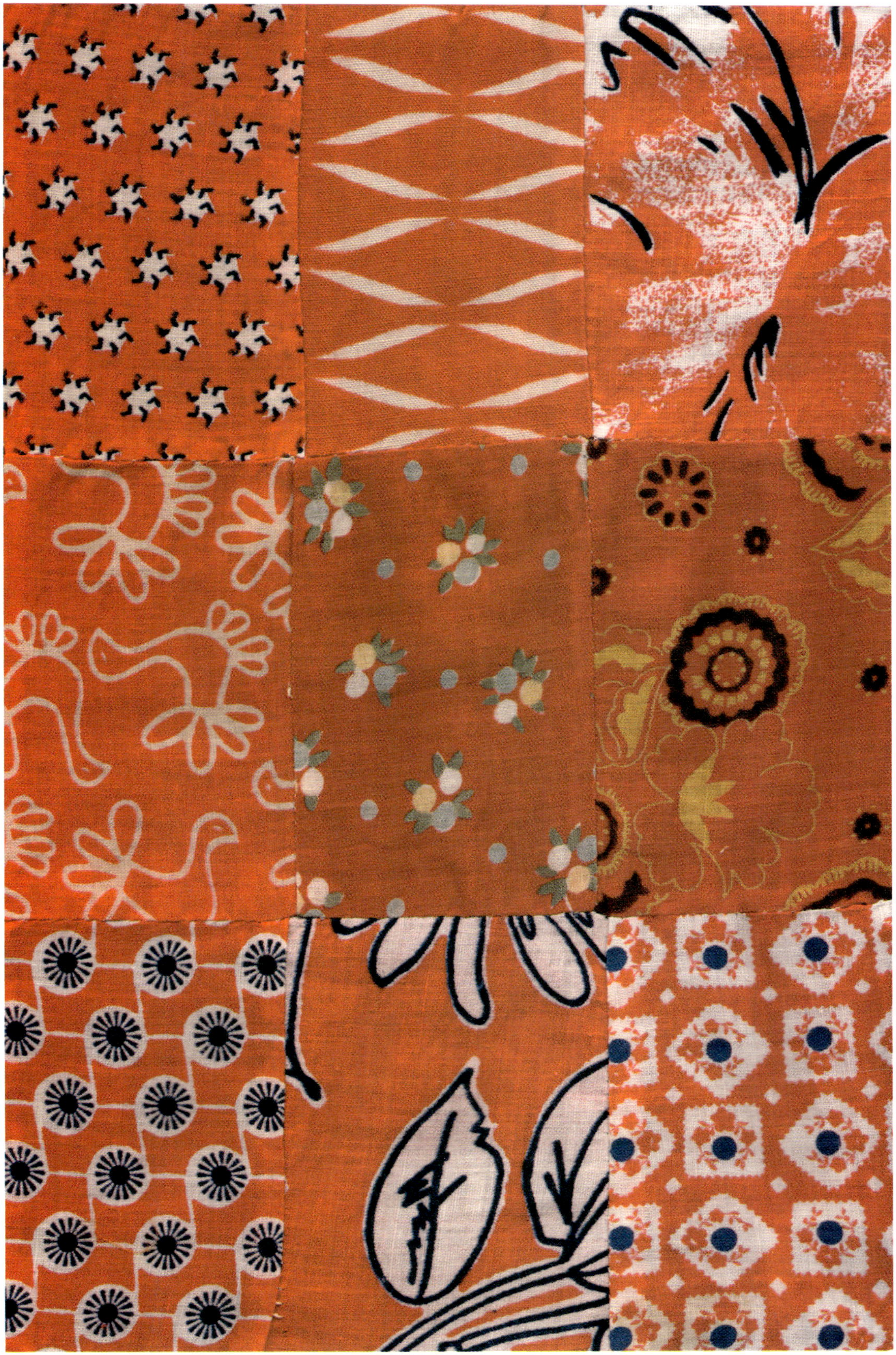

Image © Dreamstime/Yana Vergasova

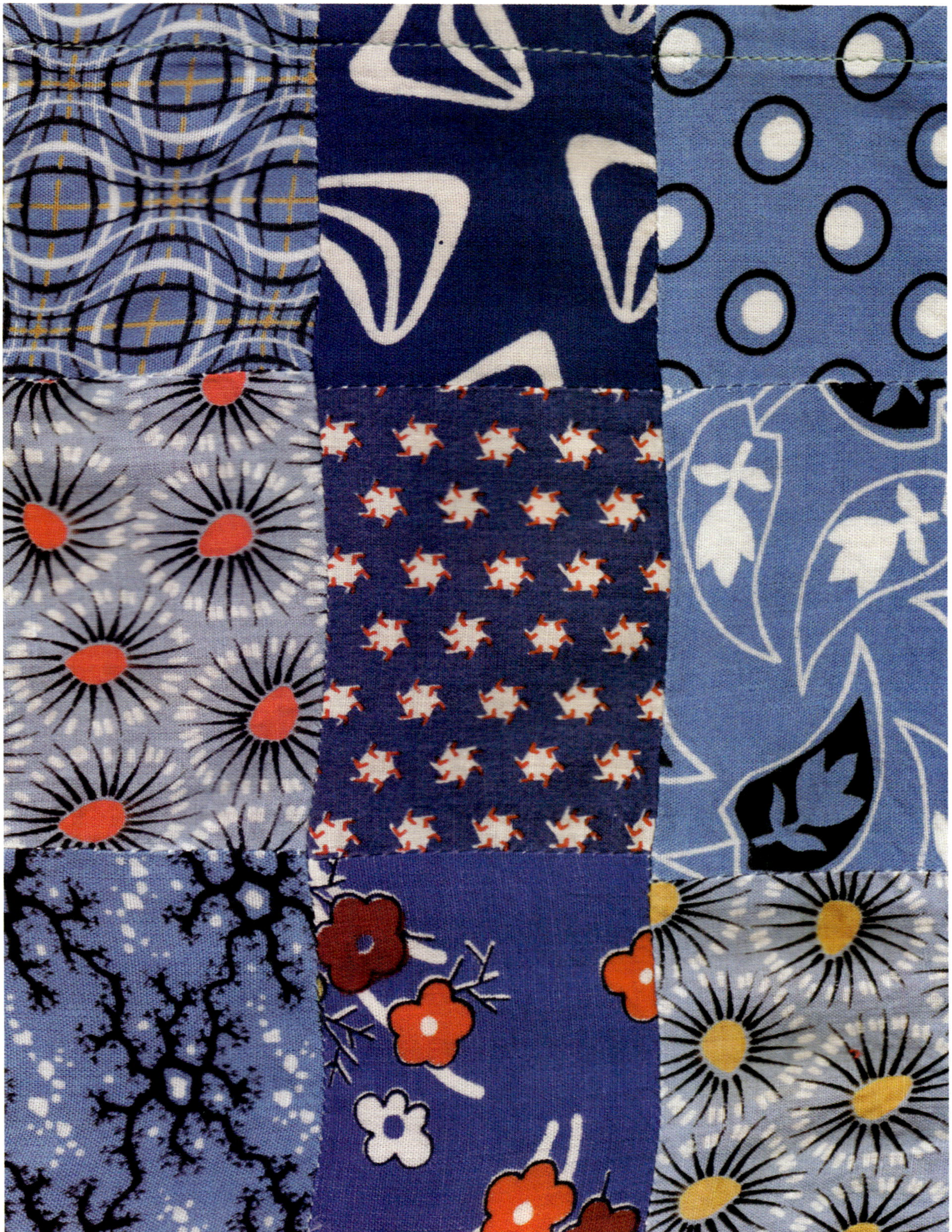

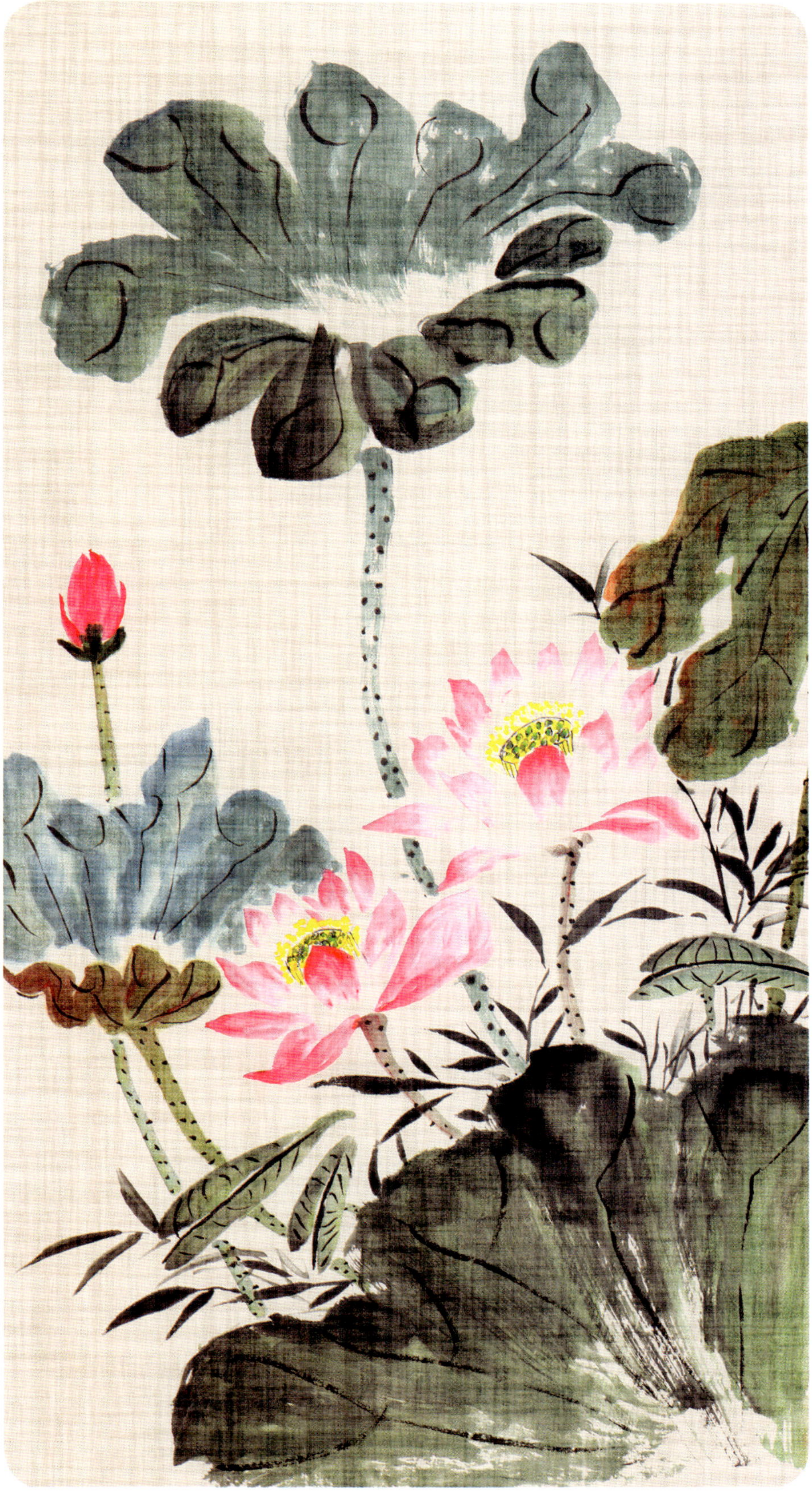

Image © Dreamstime/Shao-chun Wang

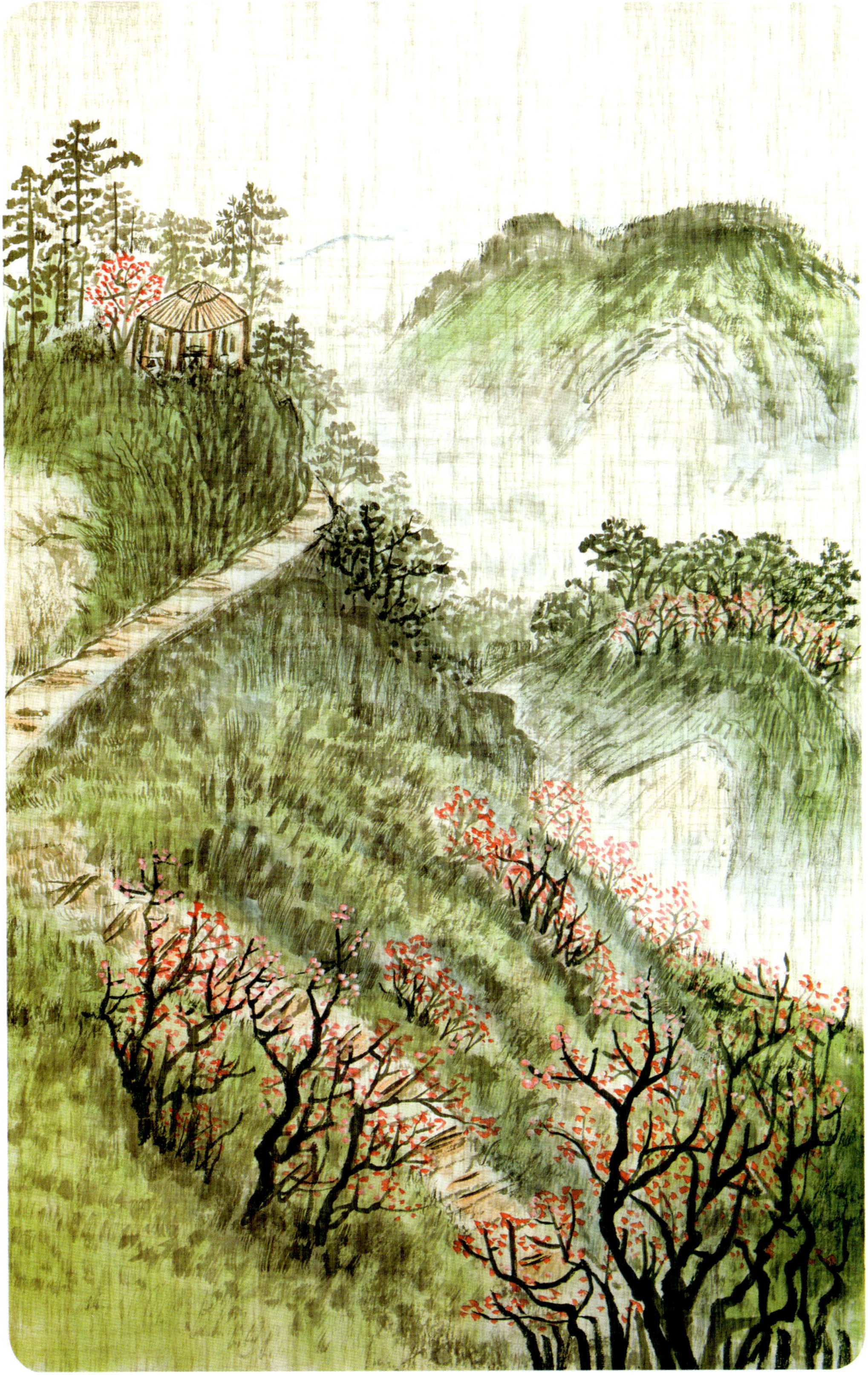

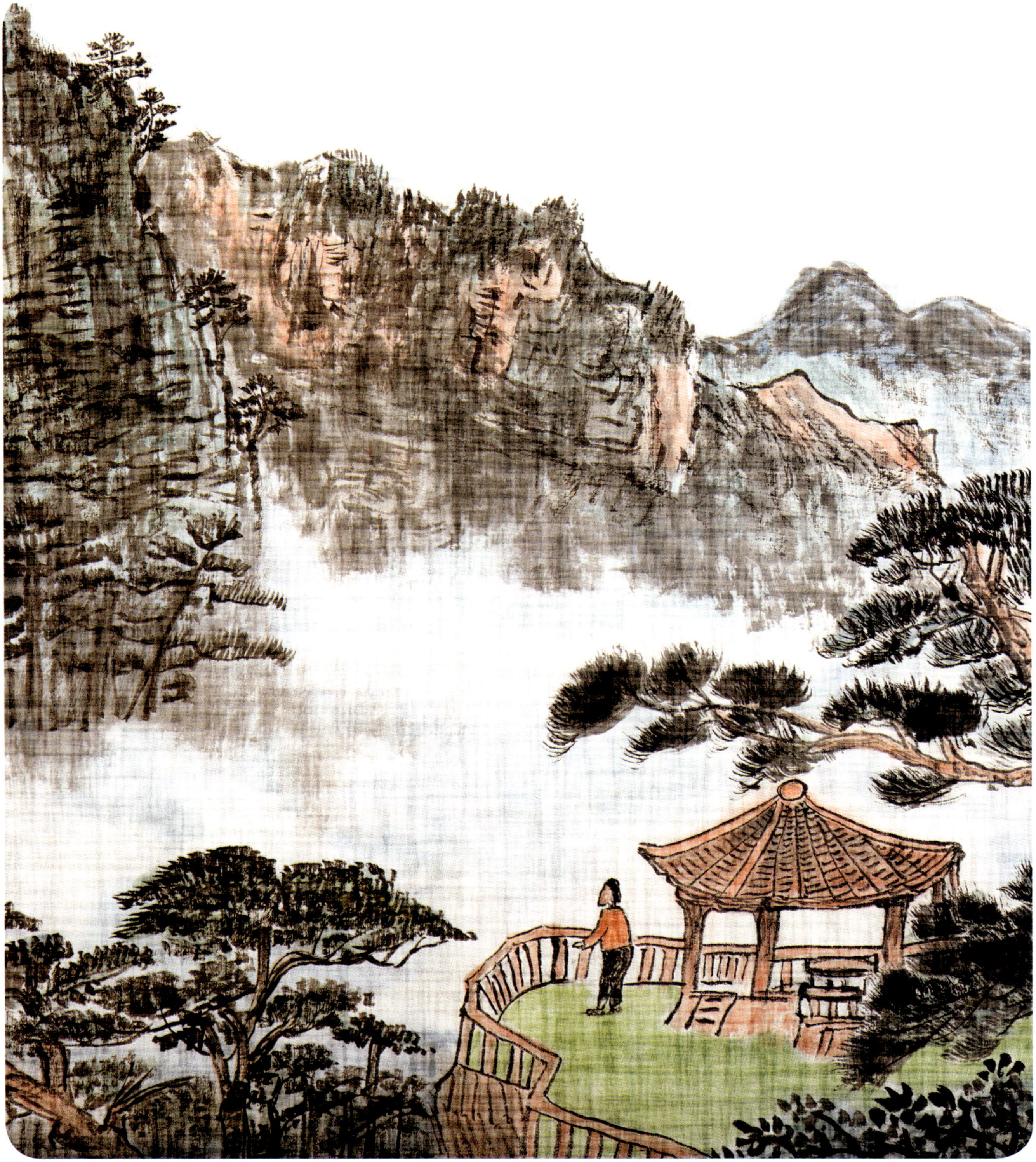

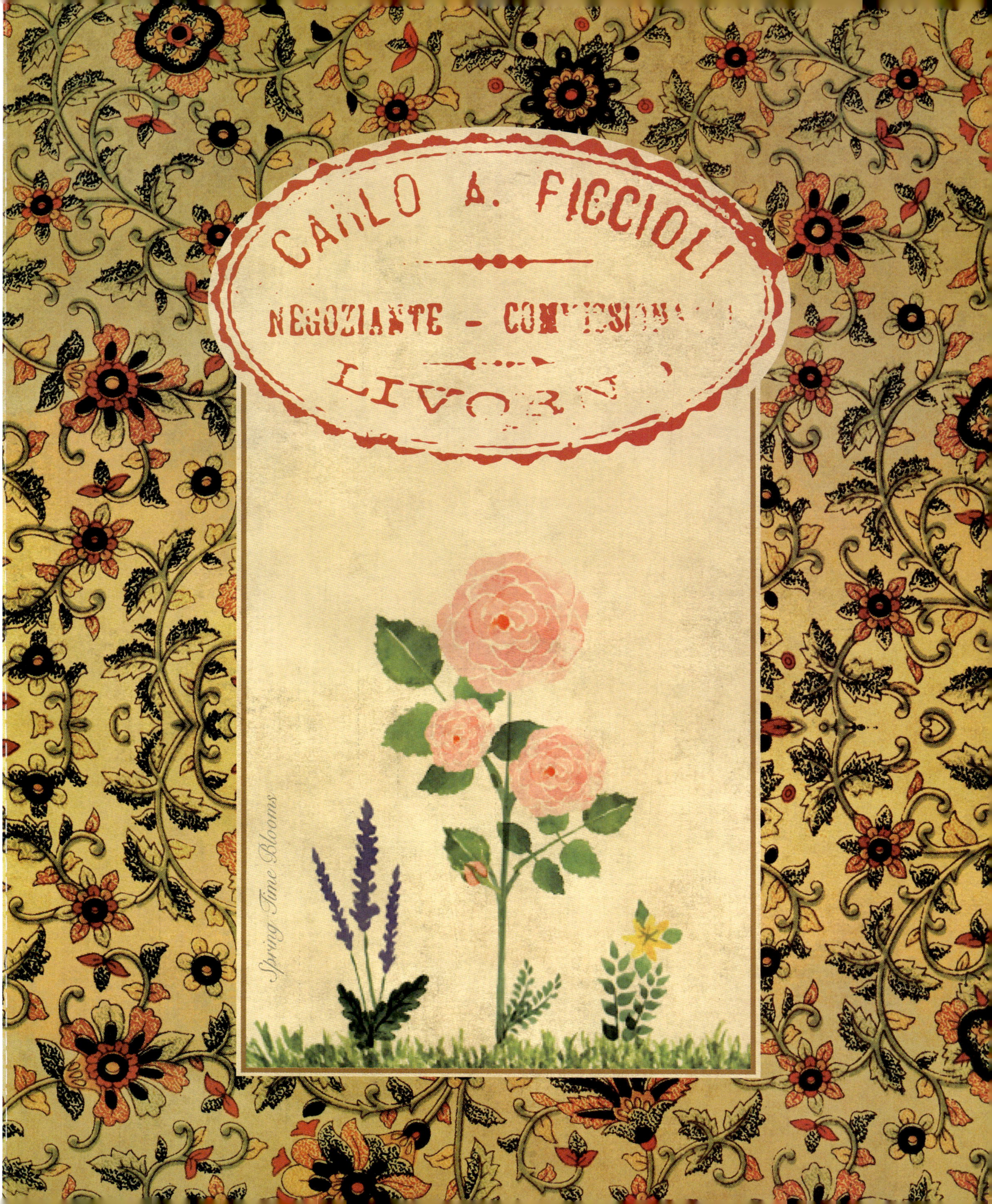
CARLO A. FICCIOLI
NEGOZIANTE
Spring Time Blooms

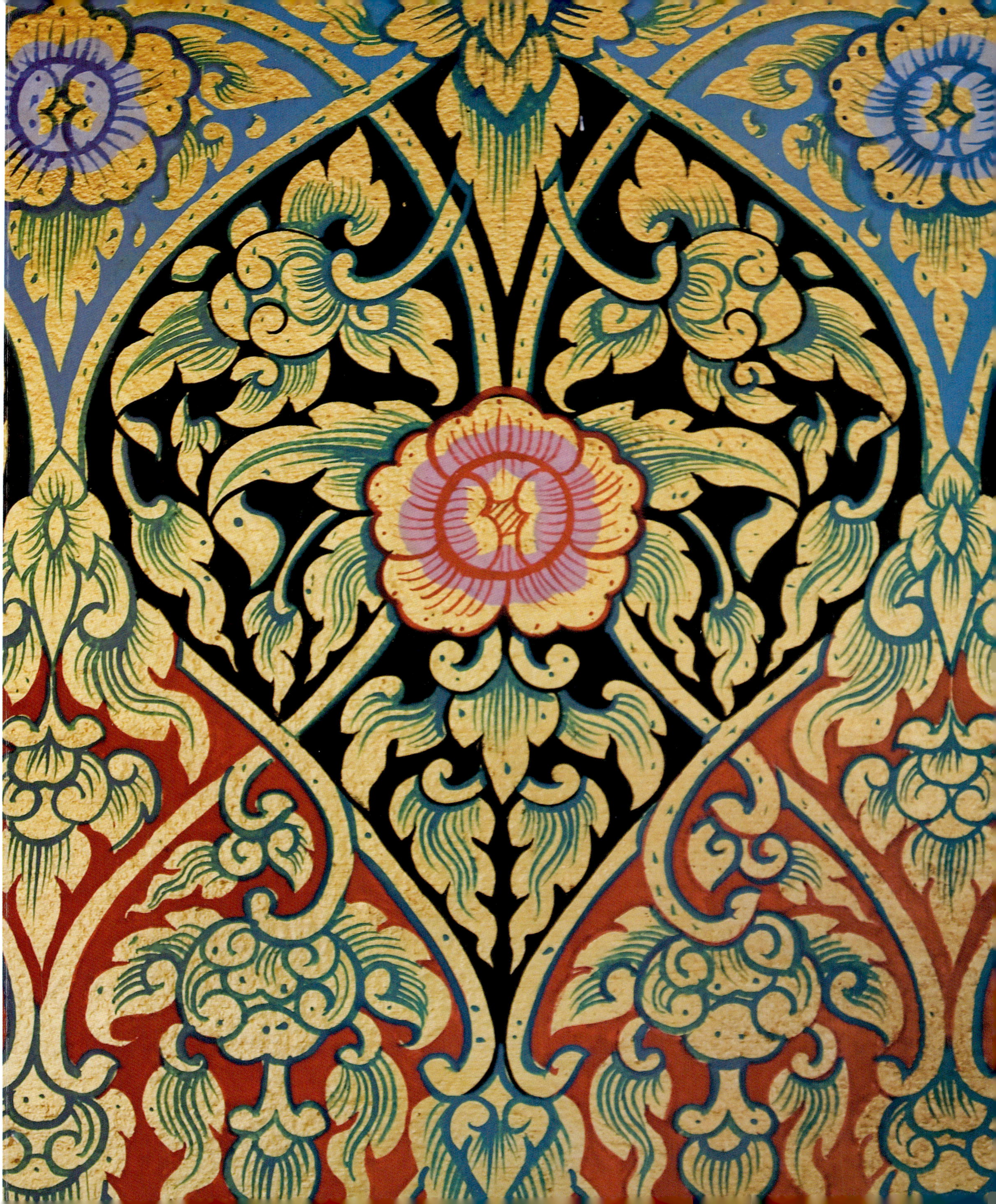

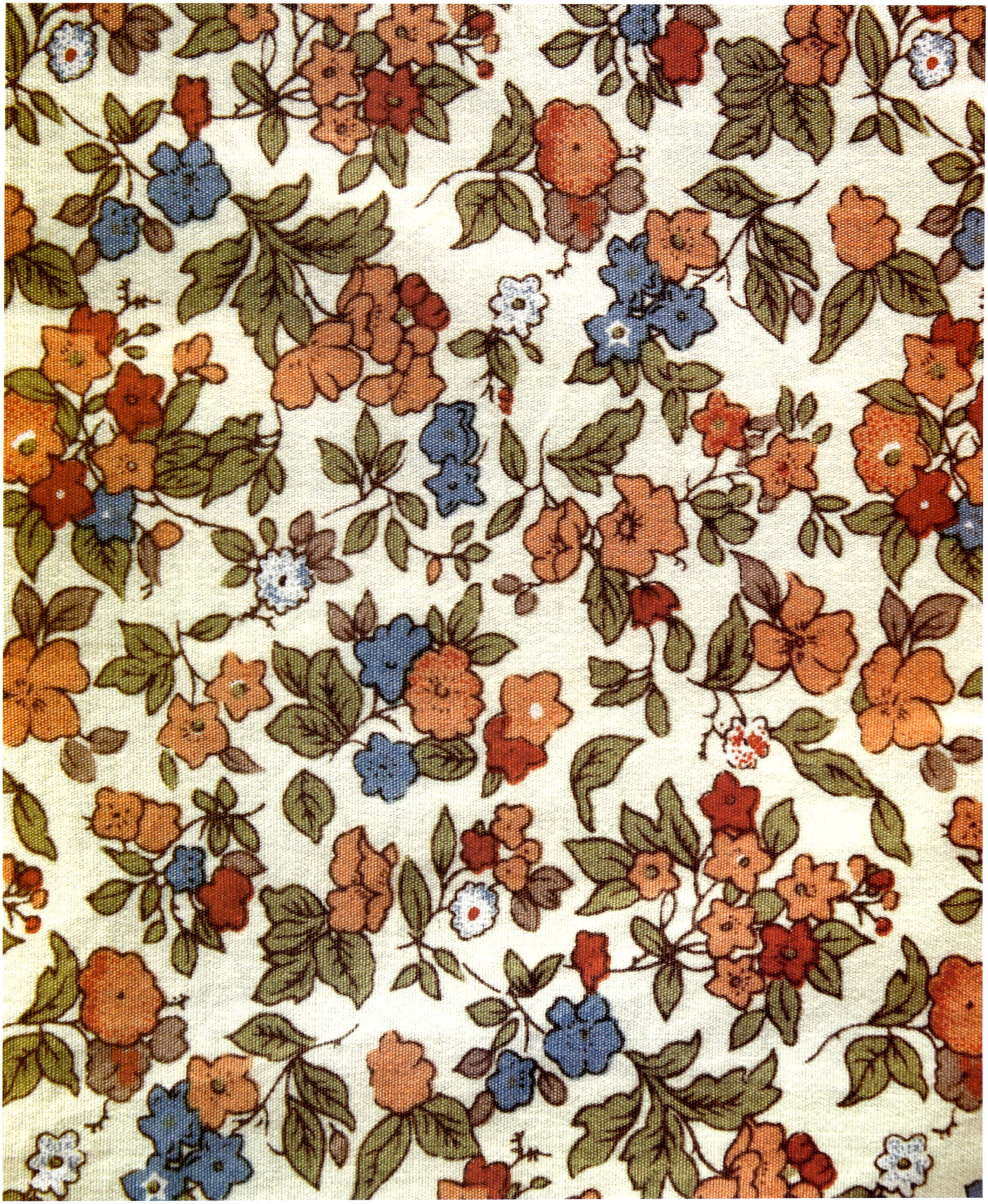

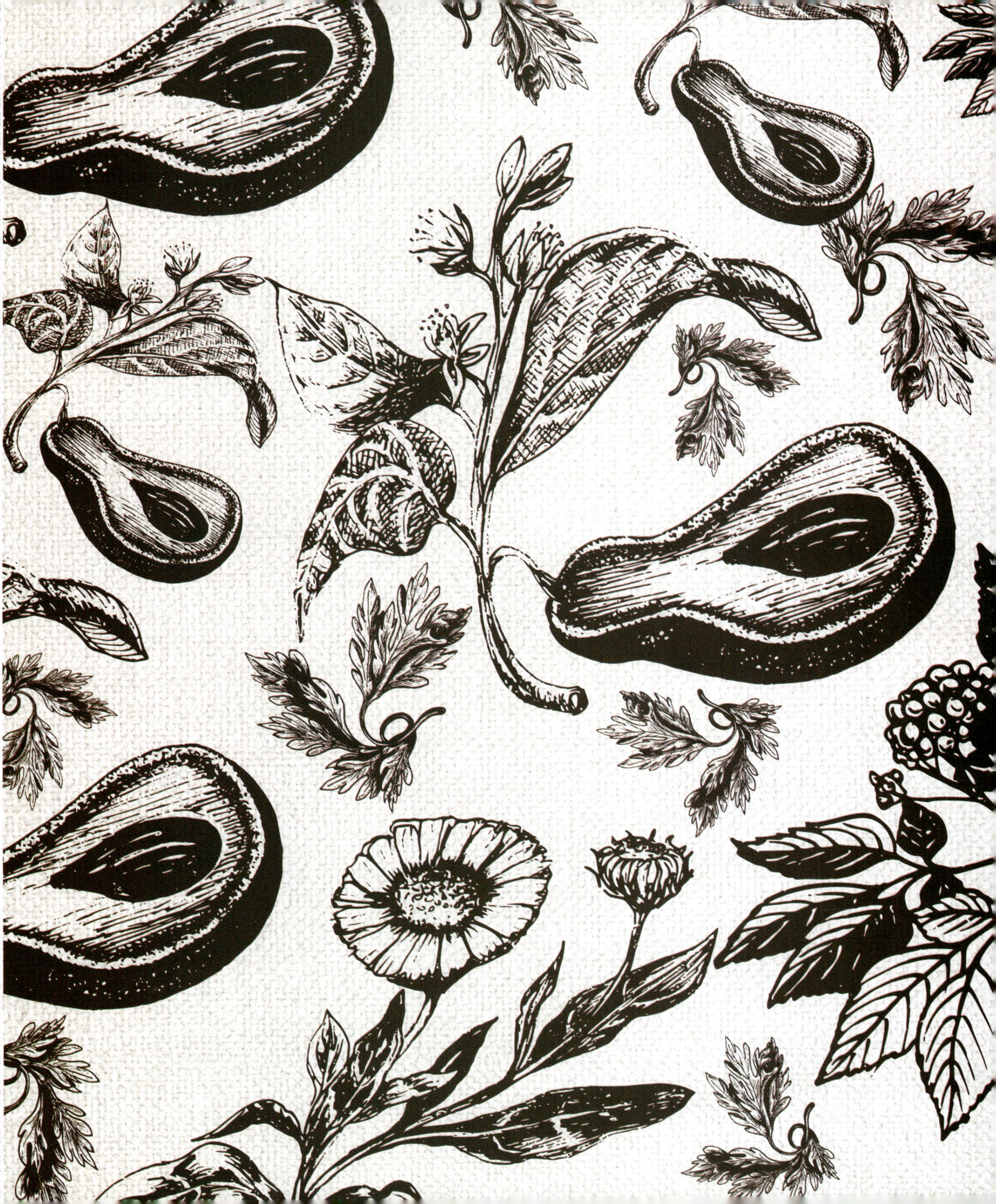

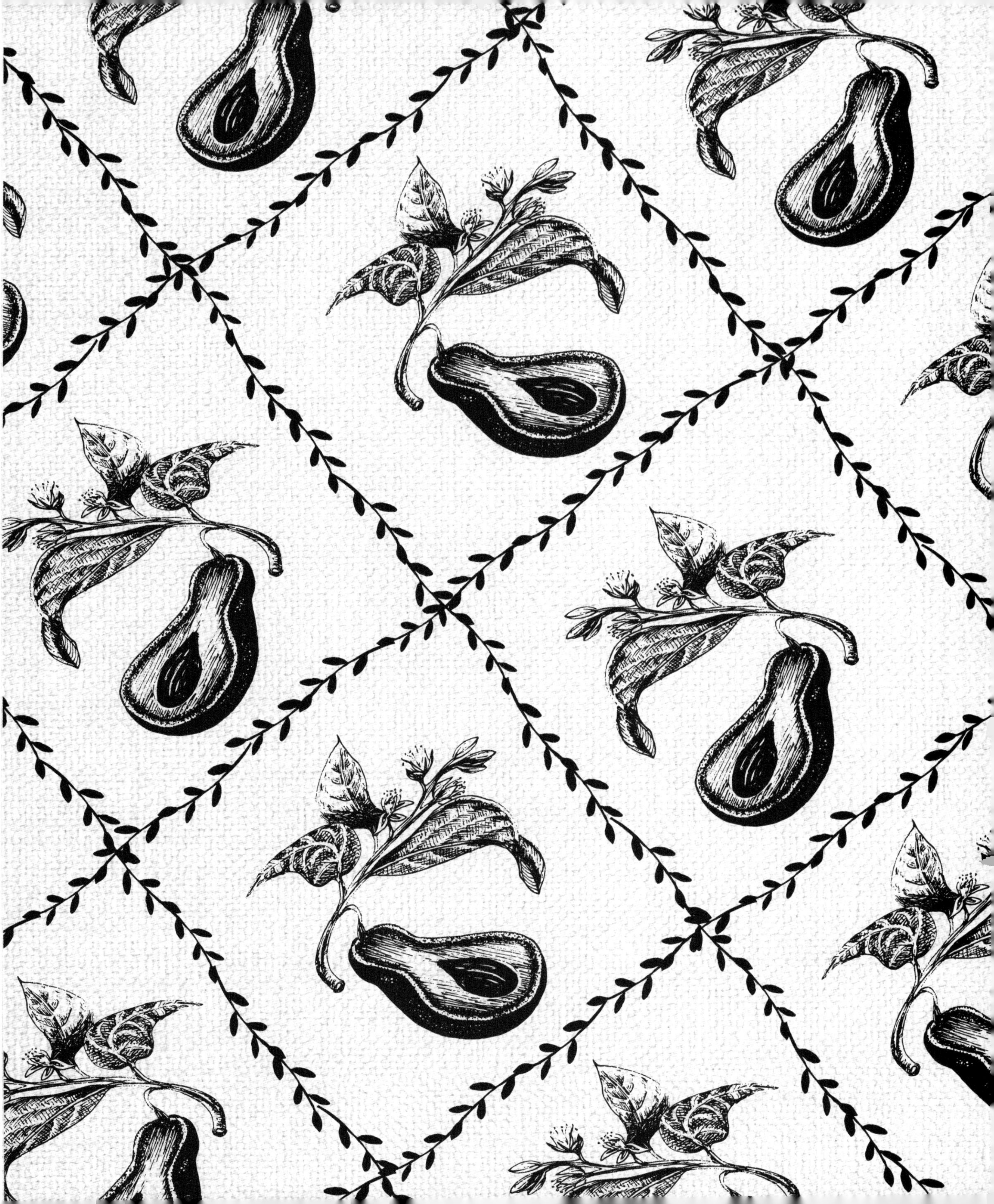

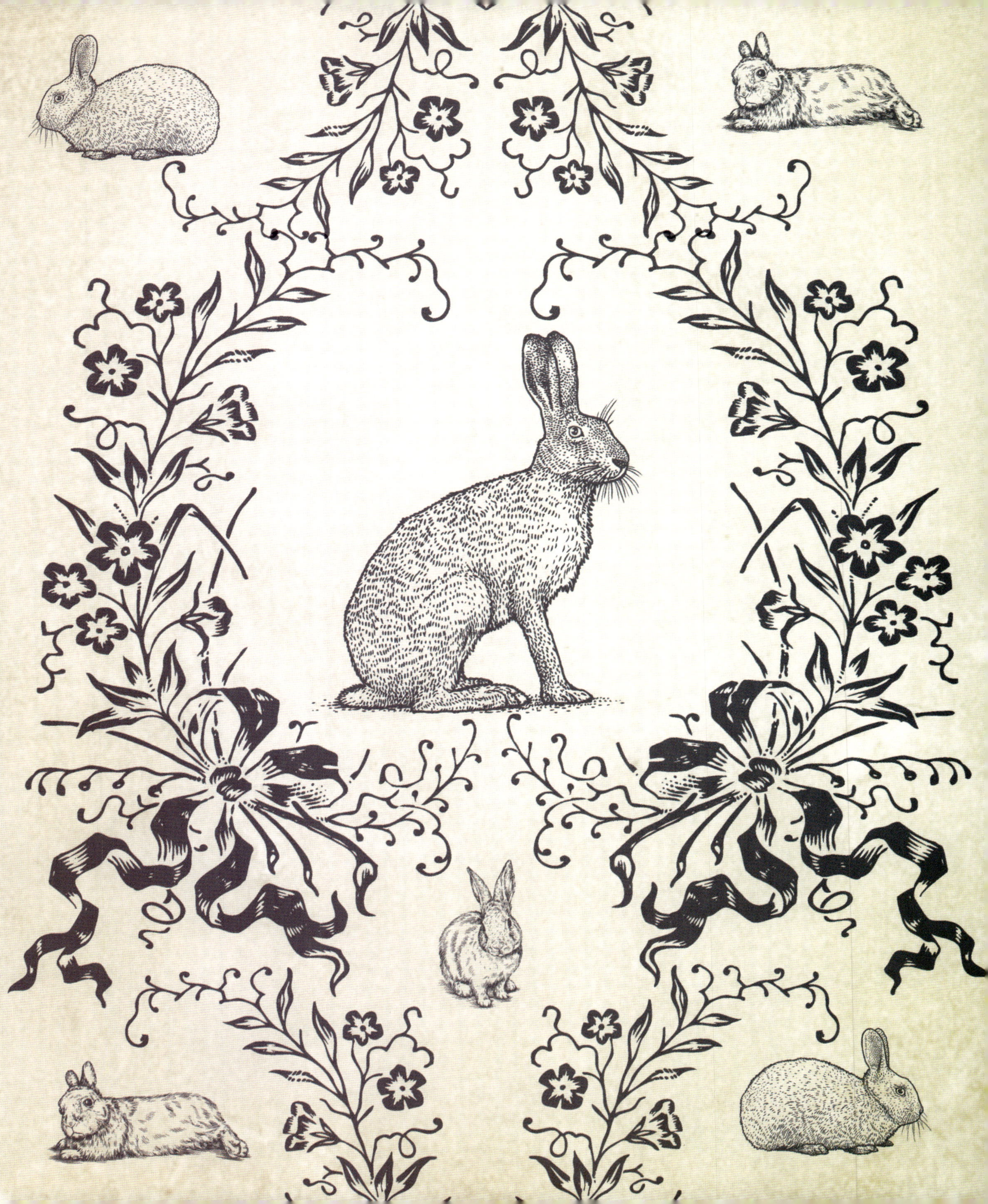

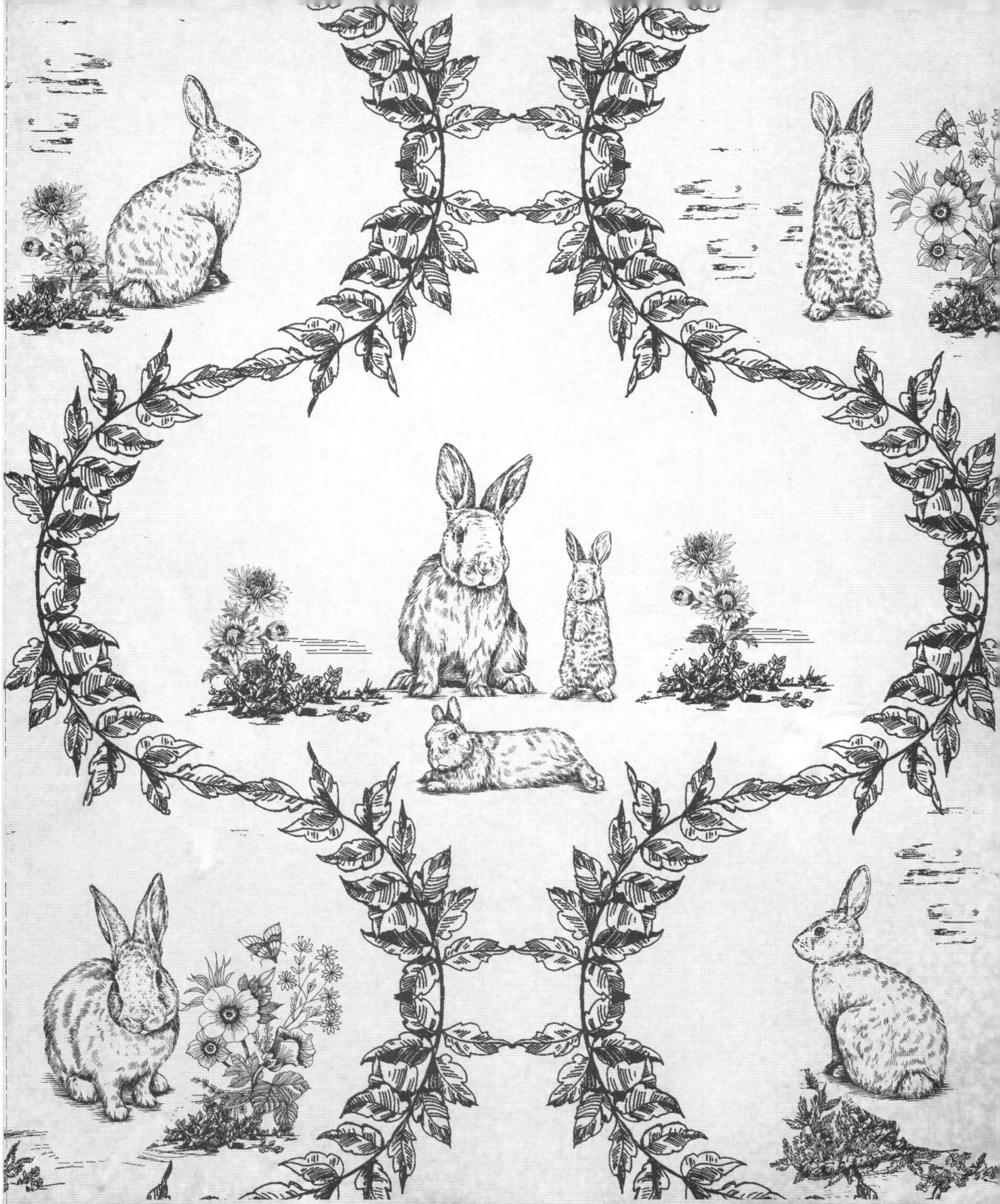

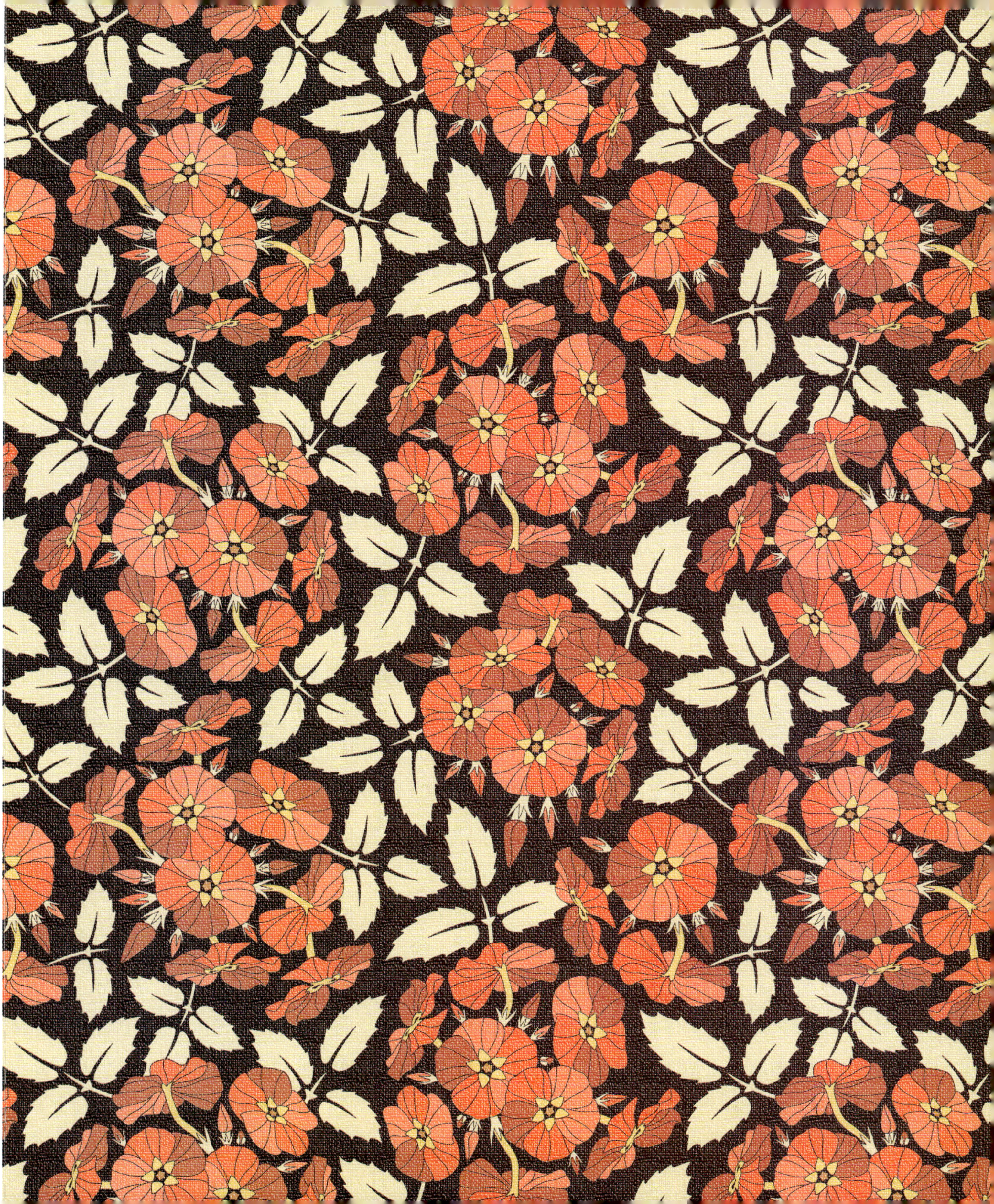

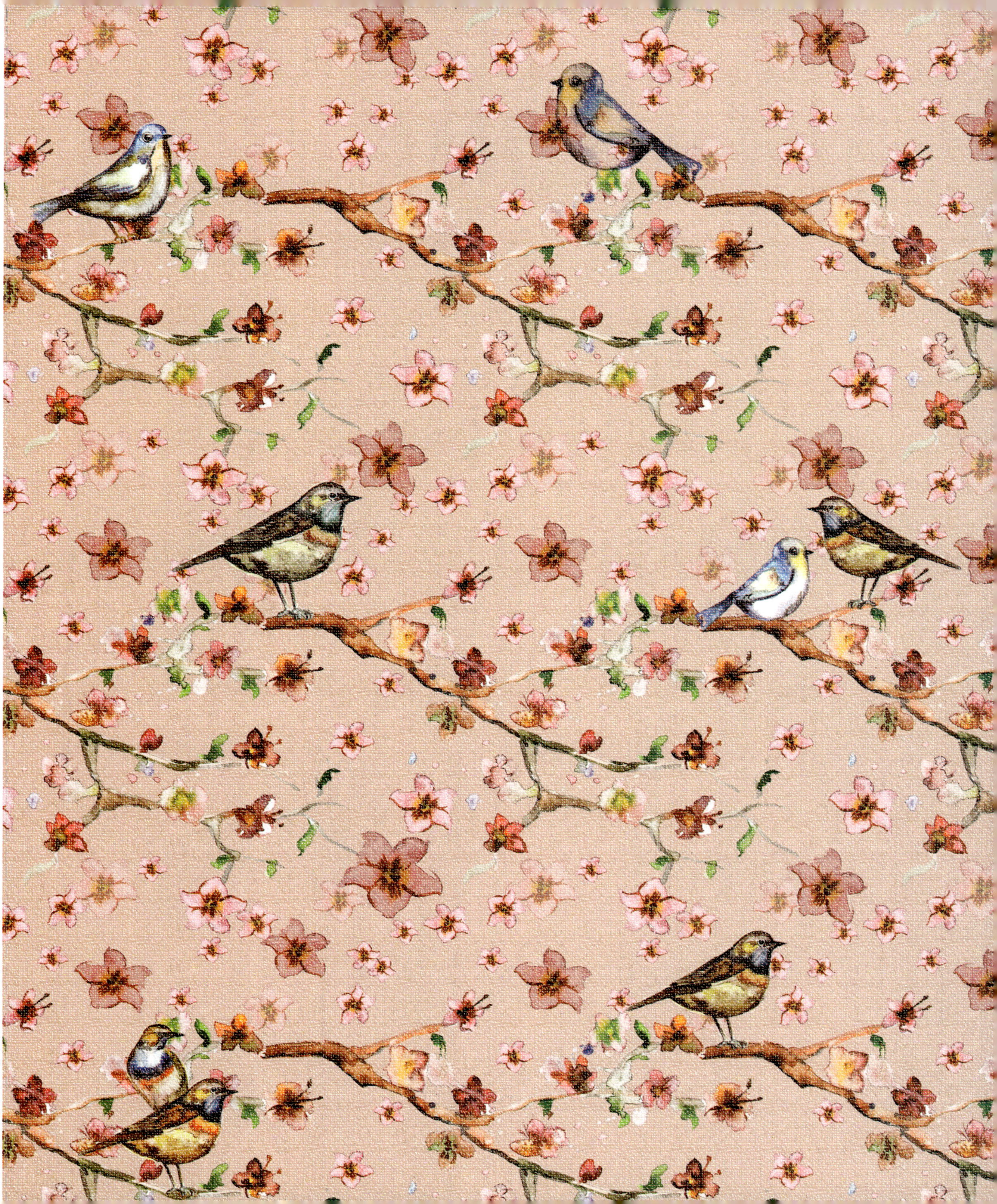

Image © 123RF/Oksana Alekseeva